Fruit growing

Roy Genders

Edited for U.S. Gardeners
By Marjorie Dietz

Pocket Gardener

Floraprint

Published 1977 by Floraprint Limited,
Park Road, Calverton, Nottingham.
Designed and produced for Floraprint by
Intercontinental Book Productions
Copyright © 1977 Intercontinental Book Productions
and Floraprint Limited. North American edition
Copyright © 1981 Intercontinental Book Productions and
Floraprint U.S.A.

ISBN 0-938804-05-7

Design by Design Practitioners Limited

Photographs supplied by Floraprint Limited (copyright
I.G.A.), Humex, Halls Homes and Gardens, Harry Hebditch,
Baco Leisure Products, Harry Smith, N.H.P.A., Spectrum
Colour Library, Bernard Alfieri

Printed in U.S.A.

Contents

1 Planning the fruit garden 4

2 Apples 8

3 Pears 16

4 Plums 21

5 Cherries 27

6 Apricots, peaches and nectarines 30

7 Grapes 33

8 Figs 38

9 Raspberries 40

10 Blackberries 43

11 Loganberries 46

12 Gooseberries 47

13 Currants 51

14 Strawberries 54

15 Blueberries and cranberries 58

16 Rhubarb 59

17 Pests and diseases 61

Index 64

1 Planning the fruit garden

Fruit-growing is a satisfying occupation and by careful planning it is possible to enjoy home-grown fruit all the year round and have sufficient in the freezer for out-of-season use.

Both dessert and culinary apples should be grown, for they are the most useful of all fruits. Where space is restricted, choose dwarf fruit trees, which usually bear sooner and are easier to care for. Ten or twelve apple trees will provide fruit from August until March if it is stored carefully.

Pears, even in standard sizes, grow upwards rather than spreading their branches, so are ideal lawn trees. They can also be grown as espaliers (horizontal-trained), on a sunny wall or along a path, and in this way will take up little space.

Of the stone fruits, peaches are the most sensitive to low winter temperatures. The blossoms that open on bare branches before the leaves unfurl are also very vulnerable to late frosts. Standard-size peach trees fit most home properties because the trees can be pruned to restrict growth. They can also be grown against a sunny wall or fence as fan-shaped trees. Full sun is essential. Reliance and Sunapee are two peach varieties that are suited to cold climates.

Most of the plums are very hardy and can be grown as part of the home orchard, as lawn trees or against a wall as fan-shaped trees. Among plums are the Damson types, used for jellies and preserves, the Gage varieties, considered superb dessert fruits as well as jam sources. In the home

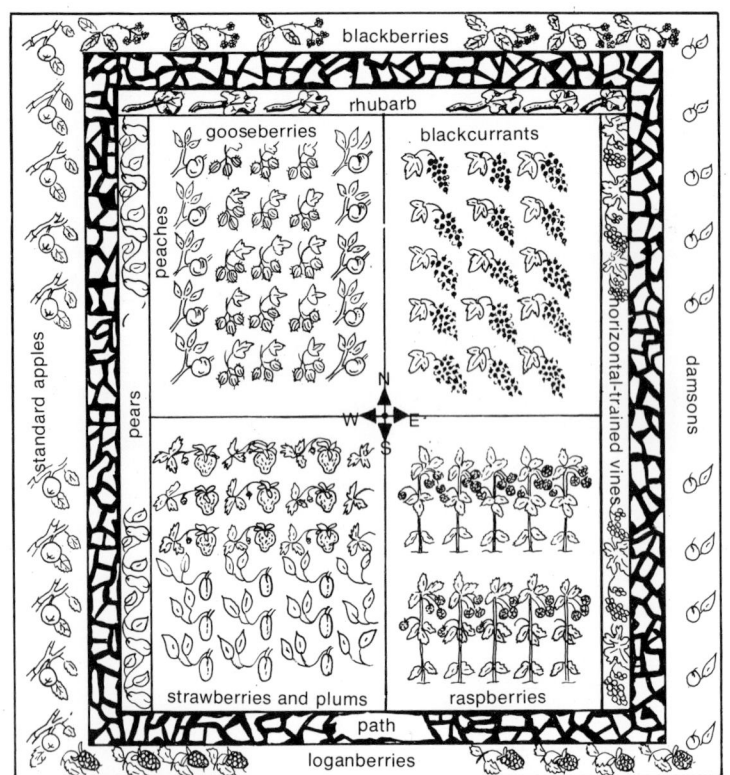

The plan makes the best use of a small area and takes into consideration the climatic aspects. For instance, on the sides where cold north-easterly winds are prevalent, blackberries are grown as a hedge and the hardy damson plums act as a windbreak. Horizontally trained grapes and pears may be planted alongside a path to conserve space; and beneath, plums and peaches, gooseberries and strawberries are grown, for they flourish in semi-shade. Red currants and raspberries are planted in full sunlight. Make the rows north to south so that all parts of the plants receive maximum sunlight.

Espalier (horizontal-trained) tree on a warm wall.

fruit orchard it is possible to intercrop among young fruit trees, especially dwarfs, with vegetable crops or other bush fruits. Examples of neat, fairly low bush fruits are currants and gooseberries. Blueberry bushes, although eventually too tall-growing for intercropping, are ornamental enough to serve as an informal hedge.

Although strawberries can be set in double rows between bush fruits, they are usually confined to their own 'bed', often at one end of the vegetable garden. While some home gardeners, mostly because of space restrictions, plant strawberries quite close together, 12 in (30 cm) it is better to set them 15–18 in (37–45 cm) apart in the row.

The cane fruits bear later than the soft fruits, and the hardiest are blackberries, which may be used as a hedge, trained along wires, or alongside a path. Varieties include Darrow, Bailey and U.S.D.A. thornless. All freeze well.

The loganberry is simply a dark red blackberry, the result of a cross between blackberry and raspberry. They also require full sun. Plant blackberries apart, raspberries at 8 ft (240 cm) 18 in (45 cm). Newburgh is an early raspberry, followed by Latham and Taylor. The autumn-fruiting varieties will prolong the season, and September and Heritage are both suitable for this purpose.

There should be a place for a grape vine, against a trellis or trained along wires.

Grape varieties vary greatly in their winter hardiness. For those in the colder regions, there are now several varieties of high quality, including Interlaken, a golden seedless variety that ripens early, and Beta, a super-hardy variety for jelly and juice.

One thing that is important today is to plant healthy, virus-free fruits. Avoid well-intentioned handouts from neighbors' gardens that may be carriers of diseases. Two sources for fruits are J. E. Miller Nurseries, Canandaigua, New York 14424 (catalog free), and the New York State Fruit Testing Association, Geneva, New York 14456. Membership in the latter is inexpensive and is refunded if orders are sent.

Apples (culinary)
Greening d
Haralson d
Mutsu d
Rome Beauty d
Wealthy d

Plums
Burbank
Damson
Green Gage
Santa Rosa
Standley d

Cherries, Sour
Early Montmore d
North Star d
Meteor d
Montmorency

Strawberries
Dunlap
Geneva e
Ogallala e
Ozark Beauty e
Sparkle

Raspberries
August red e
Cumberland
Heritage e
September e
Sodus

Peaches
Hale Haven d
Polly d
Redhaven d
Reliance d
Sun Haven d

Apples (dessert)
Golden Delicious d
Jonathan d
Macoun d
McIntosh d
Stayman Winesap d

Pears
Bartlett d
Duchess d
Maxine
Parker
Seckel d

Cherries, Sweet
Black Tartarian
Napoleon (Royal Ann)
Van d
Vista d

Currants
Red Lake
Wilder

Gooseberries
Pixwell
Welcome

Blueberries
Berkeley
Blueray
Collins
Earliblue
Lateblue

Apricots
Early Golden d
Moongold d
Moorpark d
Scout
Sungold d

Key: d – usually available as dwarf and can be grown in tubs; e – everbearing variety (bears two crops).

Types of fertilizer used in fruit cultivation.

Preparing the ground

Though each fruit requires somewhat different treatment as to soil and climate, the ground should be given a general preparation, so that if each fruit is planted at the right time, the minimum of attention will be needed to bring the soil into just the right condition for maximum crops.

Site and situation are important, for where frosts are troublesome, those fruits flowering early should be omitted unless their blossom is frost-tolerant. If you are thinking of planting only a few dwarf apple trees or a hedge of raspberries, the chances are that the correct site can be found. This means an open, sunny situation free from shade cast by buildings or nearby trees. However, if an actual orchard is contemplated, the site must be chosen with care. Here there will be a substantial investment in cost and time and starting off with the wrong site and soil conditions is folly. The wrong site might be the bottom of a slope reached by cold air draining from above, or the top of a wind-buffeted hill. Avoid any low spots where late frosts in spring can settle in and kill the flower buds. There are few fruits that will grow in wet soils – blueberries, elderberries and cranberries being the exceptions – so make certain that the soil is well-drained. Sandy soils can be improved by adding humus, as suggested below. For reliable and heavy crops, select varieties to suit the district and the soil of your garden. Blackberries require a heavy soil, containing potash. Plums and cherries do well in a limestone soil if given plenty of nitrogen; apples and pears do not, for they are often troubled by chlorosis (caused through iron starvation), in which the leaves turn yellow and the trees are stunted in growth.

Alkaline soils are usually shallow soils and need liberal amounts of humus, as do sandy soils, such as material from the compost heap, composted straw or decayed manure. If the latter is in short supply, it may be augmented by some peat or by 'green' manuring, in which seed of quick-growing plants, such as winter-rye, vetch and buckwheat, is sown thickly over the surface in fall and the plants dug in when 3 in (7 cm) high.

Except for the use suggested later in the case of heavy clay soils, adding lime to

Below: raking in fertilizer. *Opposite:* essential tools.

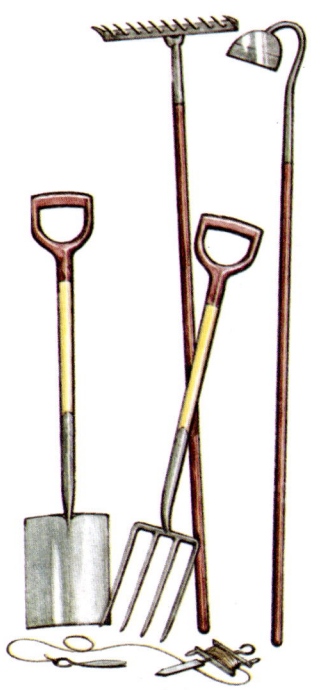

Manures and humus materials are shown here being incorporated into the trench.

When digging deep, soil is removed to a depth of at least 16 in (40 cm) or two spades' depth.

decrease the high acidity of soils is not generally recommended. If your soil is heavily acid, you may have the ideal situation for blueberries. It's a good idea to obtain the opinion of local authorities on soil problems. Your county extension agent can advise you on how to get your soil tested.

Heavy clay soil may be broken up quickly by treating it with lime obtained from a builder's supply house. If applied during the early winter just before digging the ground, the action of the lime works to break up the clay particles of the soil. Then, in March, when frost has left the ground, dig in some peat moss, compost or decayed manure before any planting is done.

Soft fruits require plenty of moisture to make growth and for the fruit to swell. To supply the plants with humus, dig in whatever materials are available, such as clearings from ditches, straw composted with an activator, leaf mold and peat. Wool and cotton waste, used hops (obtainable from breweries) and farmyard manure have the advantage over other forms of humus in that they contain greater amounts of nitrogen, which is necessary for the plants to make plenty of new growth. Other forms of nitrogenous manure are alfalfa hay, poultry manure and fish meal. Chopped seaweed is also valuable.

Working the soil

No amount of care in supplying the correct fertilizers will be of any value unless they are worked well into the soil. Clear ground is essential, for most fruits are permanent crops and it is difficult to clear the ground after planting without damaging the roots.

It is best to bring the ground into condition in autumn, while it is still dry and in a friable condition. Deep digging is necessary in order to work in the humus to a depth of at least two 'spits' or spades, about 16 in (40 cm).

As the digging is done, it is advisable to treat the ground for wireworms and millipedes, which feed upon the roots of raspberries and strawberries in particular. Everything must be done to ensure that the fruits are given the conditions necessary to bear well over a long period of time.

2 Apples

Apples are the most important of all fruit crops, for they have so many uses and can be stored or prepared for use all year. They are also the hardiest fruit, bearing well in cold climes where, apart from the gooseberry, little else would grow so well.

Apples are available as standard or dwarfs. Dwarfs can be trained to be cordons or pyramids. Although cordons take up little space, making them useful in the small garden, the training and timing to maintain these forms – and to obtain fruits – puts them beyond the ability of the average gardener. The new Malling rootstocks developed at England's Malling Station, have the ability to keep the variety grafted to it. On Malling IX, the trees will come quickly into heavy bearing. They bear fruit rather than make wood, which means growers should know how to prune them and provide the trees with a balanced diet. Dwarf trees on this rootstock may be planted 8–9 ft (240–270 cm) apart; pyramids 6–7 ft (180–210 cm); cordons 3–4 ft (90–120 cm). Plant dwarf trees 10 ft (3 m) apart; standards 15 ft (4–5 m) apart.

Trees on the dwarfing rootstocks need careful staking, for they do not produce such large roots as on the more vigorous stocks. Stake the trees immediately they are planted, using strong wooden stakes driven well into the ground, about 12 in (30 cm) from the roots and at a slight angle. Use one of the patented ties, or strips of rubber 12 in (30 cm) long cut from the inner tube of a tyre. The stake must not be in contact with the bark of the tree, or it may rub against it during windy weather.

Soil requirements

Apples require a balanced diet with plenty of humus in the soil to retain moisture – without which the fruits will not make any size and will lack juice. As apples require magnesium in the soil, it is best given, if lacking, when the ground is prepared, as magnesium carbonate, about 1 lb per sq yd (525 g per sq m). Apples also require potash; for heavy soils give 1 oz per sq yd (33 g per sq m), doubling this amount where the soil is light and the potash easily washed away. The amount of nitrogenous manures will depend on variety. The most vigorous apples will need little, for they require no assistance in making new wood. But those of more compact habit need as much compost or farmyard manure as can be obtained, and cooking apples need more nitrogen than dessert kinds. Nitrogen will intensify the green coloring of the cooking apples, whilst potash will bring out the scarlet and crimson colorings of dessert apples. Where possible, use organic nitrogenous manures, which will supply the necessary humus.

Young trees will suffer a shortage of nitrogen if planted directly into grass. In its nitrogen requirements, grass will be in competition with the trees, so it is important when planting in grass first to make a

To obtain heavy crops from limited space, plant cordons and train against wires.
Spur-forming apples may be grown in this way, or as small trees.

circle of 2 ft (60 cm) diameter and to remove the turf from this area before preparing the soil. In areas of low rainfall, all apples will benefit from a thick mulch of garden compost or farmyard manure given in June to check moisture evaporation. Trees growing in dry districts will also require more nitrogen, and if after two years they have made less than 12 in (30 cm) of new growth, give each tree a 2 oz per sq yd (66 g per sq m) application of sulfate of ammonia early in spring when growth recommences.

Lack of potash may be shown by the leaves turning brown at the edges and becoming crinkled, while the fruit will be small. Potash will also release the phosphates in the soil, which are so important in building up the size of the fruit and stimulating root action. So in spring give each tree a 1 oz per sq yd (33 g per sq m) dressing of sulfate of potash. Magnesium deficiency, which causes the leaves to turn pale green, is corrected by spraying the foliage with magnesium sulfate (Epsom salts) at a strength of 4 oz to 1 gall (25 g to 1 liter) of water.

As suggested earlier, a soil test before planting and then follow-up tests after the trees have been growing, is wise. If any of the deficiencies described above occur, consult a county extension specialist.

Standard apple trees bear heavily, but dwarf and semi-dwarf trees bear as well, and sooner.

Pollination

This is important and it is little use planting several trees of 'Macoun', just because it is one's favorite apple, without a pollinator. Since almost all apples are self-unfruitful (meaning that the pollen of another apple variety is needed for pollination), don't plan on ordering just one apple variety or several plants of the same variety. There are a few exceptions, however! The 5-in-1 apple, available as a standard (full-size) tree or dwarf, should offer no problem because five different apple varieties have been grafted on to one tree. Two other exceptions are 'Golden Delicious' and 'Rome Beauty', which tend to be self-fruitful. Generally speaking, most apple varieties will pollinate each other – *if* they bloom at the same time, that is – so the bees can work among them.

Triploids will not set their own pollen, nor will they pollinate others, so two pollinators should be grown with them to ensure heavy crops.

Planting

Apples may be planted in early spring or fall. The former is better for extremely northern regions. The soil should be in a friable condition to allow for treading it around the roots when covered over.

Select a tree with a good head and a strong sturdy stem if planting a standard. But for dwarf apples, plant maidens – i.e. one-year-old trees, which are readily established and may be trained and pruned to the requirements of the grower. They are

9

also less expensive to buy than older trees. Cordons are usually planted in trenches, made perhaps on either side of a path; the rows should be 4 ft (120 cm) apart. The trees are tied in to strong wires held in place by strong stakes at intervals of 8–9 ft (240–270 cm).

After making the hole, which must be of ample size, plant by spreading out the roots. Shorten with the pruners any that are too long. This will encourage them to make more fibrous roots. With a grafted fruited tree, especially a dwarf apple, it is important that the graft (a knobby, swollen area low on the trunk) is above ground. If it becomes covered with soil, the scion may put out its own roots, thus eliminating the desirable dwarfness of the understock. Before replacing the soil, which should contain the necessary humus and plant food, sprinkle some damp peat moss over the roots; tread in the soil as it is replaced. Fix the stake in place, tie, and water in if the soil is dry. Before doing any training, select an efficient pair of pruners that feel comfortable in the hand; the pruners will have to be in constant use.

Training and pruning

Training to the required shape will depend on the type of tree to be grown: standard, bush, dwarf pyramid or cordon.

For a **standard**, a 'feathered' tree should be obtained. This means the small 'feathers' or lateral shoots will have been removed by the nurserymen all the way along the stem. A full standard will have a 5–6 ft (150–180 cm) stem, a half standard a 3–4 ft (90–120 cm) stem. The formation of the head, which will be the same for **bush** trees, will be by one of two methods, the 'open center' plan, or the 'delayed open center'.

For the first plan, a bush tree should have a good 'leg' and, like standards, be allowed to grow unchecked the first year, during the winter 'heading' back the main shoot to 3 ft (90 cm) above soil level. This will persuade the tree to 'break' and form two or three shoots, which will form the head. Shoots appearing on the lower 18 in (45 cm) of stem with bushes should be removed. The following winter, the new shoots should be cut back to half way, and the next year the newly formed extension shoots cut back

Cordons may be used alongside a path where space is limited. Plant them 3 ft (90 cm) apart in the rows.

Dwarf pyramids give the heaviest crops in the quickest time and take up little room. Plant 4 ft (120 cm) apart.

Standards produce the heaviest crops over a long period but take several years before bearing heavily. Plant 12 ft (360 cm) apart.

Semi-dwarf trees are somewhere between the pyramid and standard forms, have a long life and bear heavily. Plant 10 ft (3 m) apart.

Spread the roots well out, removing any damaged roots before covering.

After covering with soil, tread firmly if the soil is friable, and water in if dry.

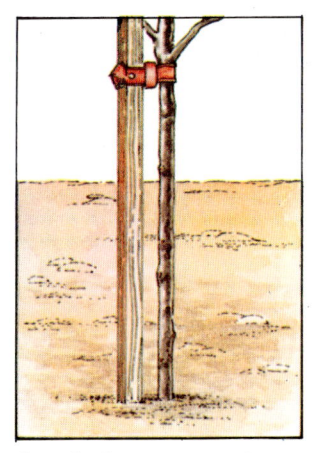

To make the tree secure, place a stake close to it and use a rubber tie.

half way, to about 9 in (22 cm) of their base. The head will now have formed.

The delayed open center is made by removing only the top 6 in (15 cm) of the main stem. Then, along the entire length of the stem, buds will form from which new growth will begin and the tree will be built up. Remove any laterals where there is overcrowding, or if several close together are facing in the same direction.

The **dwarf pyramid** form will produce the heaviest crop in the shortest time. Unlike apples in the bush and standard form, there is no waiting several years. For the tree to make as much wood and as many fruit buds as quickly as possible, bud growth must be stimulated by making a nick in the bark just above each bud on the main stem. The shoots formed from the buds are pruned back to half the new season's growth each year to encourage the formation of fruiting buds. Throughout its early life, until well established, the central main shoot must be pruned back each year. This enables the tree to concentrate its energies on the formation of side shoots.

Cordons are single-stem trees, planted at an angle of 45° to restrict the flow of sap and prevent the trees from making too much growth. Maiden trees should be planted 3–4 ft (90–120 cm) apart, and tied in to wires stretched at intervals of 12 in (30 cm) above ground. Here, the main or extension shoot should never be pruned, only the laterals, which in August should be pinched back to 6 in (15 cm) of the main stem. This will ensure the formation of fruiting spurs as quickly as possible. When the main stem has reached 6–7 ft (180–210 cm), it should be cut back to persuade the tree to direct its energies to the side shoots. The removal of surplus fruiting spurs will maintain the quality of the fruit.

The trees should be allowed to grow away in their first year untouched, to form plenty of wood while making root growth. The next winter, pruning will begin.

There are three methods: the 'established spur' system, for the more restricted or artificially trained trees; the 'regulated' system, for trees of vigorous habit; and the 'renewal' system, for keeping the tree in continuous new growth.

In the established spur system, wood formed in summer is cut back to four buds. During the following summer, the two top buds will make new growth while the lower will develop into fruiting spurs. From the cut made above the top buds, two laterals will form, which in turn should be cut back

Left: When renovating old fruit trees, use a tree saw to cut away dead wood. Remove entire branch so that the wound will callus over.

Right: To build up a healthy spur system, cut back wood formed in summer to four buds. The next year, the two uppermost buds will make new wood and the two lower buds fruiting spurs.

to two buds. Thus the balance is maintained while the tree channels its energies into making fruiting spurs. With trees over ten years old, some spur thinning is necessary to maintain the size of fruit.

The regulated system mostly applies to bush and standard trees. The idea is to keep the tree 'open' at the center by removing crossing branchlets and all in-growing laterals. Begin by shortening the laterals to a third at the end of each summer. Then cut them back as described for the spur system. The tip bearers (those that fruit at the ends of the laterals) are left unpruned until they have made excessive growth, when some wood must be removed.

The renewal system involves the replacement of old wood by new, thus maintaining the tree's vigor over many years. The side shoots are cut back to two buds from the base. These will produce two more shoots that will bear fruit. Afterwards, each is pruned back to two buds and the process continues indefinitely.

Old trees may be made more productive by removing all dead wood, using a tree saw. Where there is overcrowding at the center, entirely remove any branches, to let in sunlight. Make the cut close to the bark so that it will heal (form a callus) quickly. To leave even a few inches of the branch will enable brown rot to take hold. Paint the wound with a fungicide or with white lead paint to guard against disease.

De-horning will also increase the yield of old trees. It is the top branches that are de-horned, cutting them back by a third of their length. Make a sloping cut so that moisture will drain away, and treat with a fungicide to heal the cut as described.

If you need to restrict a certain bud, make a notch in the bark just below it. To encourage a bud to 'break' into growth, make the notch above it.

Harvesting and storing

Knowing when to harvest calls for a degree of skill. Do not remove the fruit too soon: it will keep longer if you let it stay on the tree until it is fully mature. The apples should never be ripped from the fruiting spur but gently removed with the stalk intact.

An attic, shed or cupboard is suitable for storing fruit. It must, be cool, about 40°F (50°C), dry and frostproof. Place the fruits on a layer of straw, making sure that they do not touch each other. Do not store fruit with vegetables.

Varieties

The apple varieties listed below are available as standard (full size), semi-dwarf and dwarf trees, although no one nursery is likely to offer all in every category. Some shopping around will be necessary. When buying dwarf fruits, it is sensible to ask what kind of dwarfing understock is used, since there are several and some are more dwarf than others.

It is often the case that certain varieties thrive in some areas better than others. A few varieties may not be so hardy, while others, such as the well-known Cox's Orange Pippin, are susceptible to diseases in damp areas.

Therefore, take the opportunity to consult your local nursery or horticultural advice center if you are in doubt about the best varieties for your local soil and area. Because fruit trees are a long-term crop, do select the right varieties.

Beacon Not of the highest quality, but recommended for far north regions. Ripens early, bears heavily, has good red color and is not as perishable as some early apples.

Cortland Known for both dessert and culinary qualities. A large red-striped fruit with white flesh. For storage, pick five days after McIntosh.

Cox's Orange Pippin One of the most popular apples ever introduced. It is a weak grower, susceptible to frosts, and bears well only where everything is in its favor. Yet the fruit has a more subtle blending of aromatic flavor and crispness than any apple, and is good for eating from fall to late winter. Not generally available from nurseries.

Left: In the regulated system of pruning (mostly for semi-dwarf and standard trees) crossing branchlets and in-growing laterals are removed to keep the tree open at the center. Shorten the laterals to a third at the end of summer, then cut back the laterals as for the spur system. Leave the tip bearers unpruned until they have made excessive growth, then remove some of the wood.

Above: In the renewal system of pruning, old wood is replaced by new to maintain vigor. Cut side shoots back to two buds from the base. These will produce two more shoots, which will become fruit-bearing. Then prune each back to two buds, and so on.

13

July Red Early summer apple for most of the Northeast. Fruit is blush colored with red splashed stripes. A new variety that is much praised for its eating quality and superior keeping properties for an early variety.

Left: One of the best dessert apples, Cox's Orange Pippin is offered in both dwarf and standard-size trees by a few fruit specialists.

Fireside A very hardy apple for Minnesota, North Dakota and like climates. Fruit is red and large, juicy, sweet and crisp, and keeps well. A late variety that stores for three months.

Golden Delicious Retains its popularity and, with its evenly shaped fruit and clear yellow skin, it is a favorite of the supermarkets. A high quality fruit.

Haralson Deep red apple that stores for 4–6 months. Late variety recommended for cold climates.

Jonagold An apple prized for dessert and culinary qualities. Attractive fruit has scarlet stripe over a yellow background. Good keeper – until spring at storage temperatures of 33°F (1°C). Will probably replace Golden Delicious.

Macoun Outstanding dessert apple, red and of medium to small size (hand or chemical thinning may be necessary to prevent over-bearing and small fruits). Reminiscent of McIntosh in its crispness, but better flavored. Popular in the Northeast.

McIntosh One of the most popular dessert varieties, famous for its sparkling red color and crisp white flesh.

Below: A well spaced and heavily laden branch, the result of good pruning and cultivation.

Right: Golden Delicious, one of the most reliable dessert apples, bears heavily in both dwarf and standard trees.

Mutsu A very large yellow apple that is late. Fine dessert and culinary qualities. One large fruit can yield a bowl of sauce.

Spigold A triploid, so can neither pollinate itself or other varieties. A red-striped, very large apple, excellent for cooking uses.

Wealthy A fine apple known for its hardiness. The fruit is yellow and striped with scarlet. It makes excellent eating right from the tree in the fall and also cooks well.

Winter Banana A variety for the South and mild climates of the West Coast. Fruit is large and pink-fleshed.

3 Pears

Natives of the warm regions of the Mediterranean, pears require greater warmth than apples for the fruit to ripen correctly and so attain their full flavor and keeping qualities. Pears require the sunniest places in the fruit garden, where they may be grown as standards or bush trees, and in the pyramid and cordon form, requiring similar culture to the apple in their pruning. However, if pruning is neglected, pears continue to bear well. Pears are at their best where grown as espaliers or in horizontal tiers, the arms being either fastened to a wall or to strong galvanized wires supported by posts at intervals of 8 ft (240 cm). Espaliers may be grown in the open, possibly alongside a path, or to divide one part of the fruit garden from another.

Espalier trees

A maiden tree will form one pair of arms each year, which can be grown on to any length. Espaliers can also grow to any height and will often be seen covering the entire wall of an old house to a height of 30 ft (9 m) or more. Long ladders must then be used for picking fruit and pruning at the top. In the garden, the topmost arms should be about 7–8 ft (210–240 cm) from soil level so that cultivation can be readily carried out.

After planting the young tree, make a nick in the bark above two buds, one on either side of the stem and pointing in opposite directions, to make them 'break'. These will form the first arms or tier. The leader shoot is allowed to grow away. Next season, in early spring, another two buds are selected on either side of the stem, and so on, selecting a pair of buds each year that are spaced about 16–18 in (40–45 cm) above each other.

At first, the new wood growing from the main stem will tend to grow upwards. It is advisable to fix canes to the wires, first at an angle of 45°, to which the shoots are fastened. The canes are gradually brought to the horizontal position, then fastened to the wires.

The first tier will grow to about 3 ft (1 m) on either side of the main stem in a year. The following year, early in August, to encourage the formation of fruiting spurs, which will bear fruit the next year, all shoots growing from the arms should be pinched back to 4–5 in (10–12 cm) of the main stems. The plant will then form fruiting buds instead of making excess wood. As the arms continue to grow, at the end of each summer, cut back the new season's wood to about half way, to a bud that will form the extension shoot to grow on next year. This process may continue for several years, until the arms are approximately 6 ft (180 cm) in length; therefore, with espaliers it is desirable to plant them about 12 ft (3·5 m) apart.

As pears bloom about two weeks before apples, many varieties should not be planted in frost-troubled gardens unless they are planted against a warm wall. Varieties for colder regions have been developed by the University of Minnesota and the South Dakota State University, and include Parker, Patten and Luscious. The disease fire blight can be serious with pears.

Pollination

Pollination is as important for pears as for apples. Though several will be in bloom at the same time, they are unable to fertilize each other. The fertile Conference is unable to pollinate Beurré d'Amanlis; neither will Seckel fertilize Louise Bonne. They need another pollinator, such as Marguerite Marillat or Durondeau.

Certain pears, such as Duchess, are self-fertile, setting fruit with their own pollen, but they will set heavier crops with another in bloom at the same time. The variety

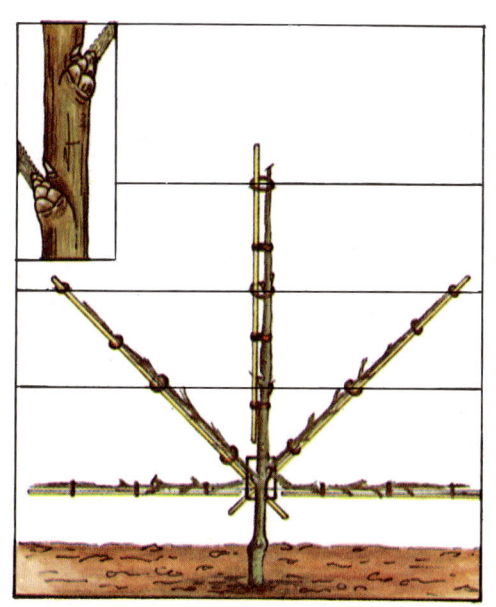

Opposite: Doyenne du Comice, also known as Comice, requires a warm garden. It is one of the most popular of the dessert fruits.

Above: Buds on fan trees can be induced to develop or remain dormant by nicking either above or below the buds.

Gather pears dry, before they're frosted.

Wrap in greaseproof paper, stand on end.

Magness has sterile pollen and should be planted with Duchess for cross-pollination to set fruits.

Early and mid-season varieties, and mid-season and late pears may be planted together, for their flowering times will overlap. Thus Conference and Bartlett will fertilize each other. However, two superior pear varieties that might appear to be a suitable planting combination in the home fruit garden, Bartlett and Seckel, will *not* fertilize each other. A third variety must be included.

Rootstocks

There are several rootstocks for pears that are grafted on to quince stock. Quince B is comparable to MII of apples, making large trees that crop heavily but take longer to come into bearing than the more dwarf stocks (such as Quince C, which is used for pyramids and cordons). Also, those pears that are slow to begin cropping, e.g. Comice and Beurre Hardy, should be worked on this stock. Quince A comes somewhere between these two stocks and is the rootstock mostly used.

Where a large standard tree is required, pears are worked on wild pear stock and this is also used for the weaker growers. It is the most vigorous rootstock.

Trees on quince stock must be planted with the graft at least 3 in (8 cm) above soil level so that scion rooting does not occur. Dig a large hole so that the roots can be spread out well, making it a depth such that the graft is comfortably above the soil after treading down. Sprinkle peat moss over the roots and mix in compost before replacing the soil, treading it well down. Then stake the trees as for apples.

Pruning

As to their pruning, pears are divided into two sections: those of vigorous upright habit, and those of weaker, drooping habit. In the former group are Comice, Conference, and Bartlett.

When pruning, the upright growers should be cut back to an outward-facing bud and the droopers to an upward bud. This will correct the 'drain-pipe' habit of the second, weaker group and the 'umbrella' habit of those of the first group. Those of weeping habit are mostly tip bearers and light croppers and so require little pruning.

Each shoot or lateral will form both fruiting and wood (foliage) buds. The latter lie flat along the stem and are more pointed. Several years after planting, the spur bearers may need to have some of their spurs removed so as to maintain the size and quality of the fruit.

Harvesting and storing

Pears require more care in their harvesting than apples. They bruise easily and are harmed by frost, while they deteriorate quickly if overripe. They will be ready to gather if, when you take the fruit on the palm of the hand and lift it, it parts from the spur with its stem attached. They require a temperature of 45°–50°F (7°–10°C) to store well and should be kept in a darkened room or a cupboard or drawer. Pears will sweat and quickly deteriorate in a too cold place, such as a refrigerator. However, if they are carefully stored, some pears will keep until Easter.

Varieties

When selecting the varieties, remember to choose varieties that fruit at different times. Nothing is more annoying than to wait all year for fresh pears, then to have them all at once and many of them to be wasted. Most catalogs will give an indication as to the expected date of fruiting.

Aurora Bright yellow pear with russet blush. Large with juicy, aromatic flesh that is sweet. Early (late summer in most Northern regions), the fruit storing well until early winter. Vigorous tree but not resistant to fire blight.

Bartlett Possibly the best all-round pear ever raised. It makes a compact tree and bears heavily, the white flesh retaining its quality after preserving. It ripens early (mid- to late summer) but is not resistant to fire blight.

Beurre d'Anjou Large, greenish fruits considered comparable to Comice in quality. Hardy to southern Vermont and like regions. Late ripening; the fruit stores well into winter in a cool cellar. Moderately resistant to fire blight.

Beurre Hardy The rose-tinted flesh has a pleasant rose perfume. It makes a strong, upright tree. Hardy. Offers some resistance to fire blight.

Clapp's Favorite An old pear of vigorous, upright habit. It bears heavily, the pale yellow fruit, striped crimson, ripening early (midsummer). A good pollinator and resistant to fire blight.

Colette The large fruits are yellow with a red or pink blush and are of superb quality. Very hardy. The fruits ripen over several weeks, beginning in mid- to late summer. Vigorous but not resistant to fire blight.

Conference Although well known to pear fanciers, finding a source for this variety may be difficult. It is hardy, a valuable

Possibly the best all-round pear ever, the Bartlett makes a compact tree and bears heavily. The flesh retains its quality after canning.

pollinator and known for its reliable harvests. The dark green fruits, heavily russeted, are of excellent flavor.

Doyenne du Comice This is the finest of all pears, its melting cinnamon-flavored fruit having no equal. It requires warmth and a long growing season, conditions best met in a few regions of the Pacific Coast.

Duchess A famous French pear nearly as revered for its flavor as Comice. The russet fruits are ripe in fall. This is a hardy variety resistant to fire blight.

Gorham Forms a neat, upright tree that is slightly resistant to fire blight. The fruits are bright yellow, similar to Bartlett, and fine for dessert or canning.

Magness Green-yellow fruits, slightly russeted, juicy and sweet. Ripens about 3½ weeks after Bartlett. Its pollen is sterile, but it is highly resistant to fire blight.

Maxine A yellow pear with a rating of only fair quality, its flesh being coarse. It is hardy and ripens late. It is quite resistant to fire blight, an important asset.

Moonglow Pale yellow fruits that ripen before Bartlett, but are rated as being of only medium quality. Very resistant to fire blight.

Parker Fruits, which are somewhat similar to Bartlett, ripen in early fall. It is a very hardy variety recommended for Minnesota and like climates. Patten is very similar, but later.

Seckel A small brown pear of magnificent flavor. Ripens in early fall. Resistant to fire blight.

Sirrine Yellow fruits slightly blushed of high dessert quality, being sweet and juicy. Bears about the same time as Bartlett but is much more resistant to fire blight.

Conference is a pear famous for its quality among fruit fanciers. It is a valuable pollinator.

4 Plums

After apples, plums are the next most widely grown fruits, for they have both dessert and culinary uses. Plums do not keep for long but, by planting for succession, they may be enjoyed from early summer to fall.

Americans are fortunate in having a wide choice among plums. There are the best varieties from Europe, including the famous Green Gage and Damson types, the Japanese varieties, and various native species and hybrids. These plums all vary, not only in their fruits, but also in their hardiness and tolerance of climatic differences. The prune is a kind of plum. Commercial production of prunes is concentrated in California and a few other Western states where the proper conditions for drying the fruits exist.

Some of the native plums make small trees or shrubs and even some standard-size plums such as Green Gage possess a habit dwarf enough for a small garden. However, some European plums are grown on dwarfing understock. Both the dwarf and standard plum comes quickly into bearing.

The Damson is such a special plum that

Plums can be enjoyed from early summer to fall.

Left: Root pruning restricts the growth of plums without fear of 'bleeding'. Scrape away soil to 4 ft (120 cm) and remove the most vigorous roots with a sharp knife or cut with a spade.

Opposite: If removed with their stalks, plums will keep for several weeks in cotton.

it deserves extra attention, if only to forestall its neglect by future plum growers. The trees are among the hardiest of fruits and able to bear heavy crops when growing in shallow soil and rocky outcrops. For cold, exposed gardens they will bear more heavily than most other plums. However, when provided with moderately fertile soils containing moisture-retentive humus in the form of peat moss, compost, leafmold, decayed straw or whatever is available, the size and quality of the fruit will be much enhanced. They will need almost no pruning, as they make only small twiggy growth. Although considered self-fruitful, damsons will bear better if another European plum is planted nearby. Damsons are not suitable for eating out of hand, but they make delicious preserves and pies with their own unique flavor. Planting distances for standard trees is about 8–10 ft (2½–3 m) apart.

Training and pruning

It does not require the same degree of pruning attention as either the apple or pear. The plum fruits mostly on the new wood and, apart from the removal of any dead wood, excessive pruning must be avoided. Stone fruits suffer from 'bleeding', which weakens the tree and enables disease, especially silver leaf, to enter where cuts or wounds have been made.

In spring, cut back any unduly long shoots, and early in July, pinch back to half way all side shoots, which will have made new growth. Plums form their fruit buds along the entire length of the branches and a well-grown tree may be allowed to carry a greater amount of wood than any other top fruit.

The pyramid, budded on to the dwarfing St Julien A stock, is ideal for small gardens. Maiden trees are planted 8–9 ft (240–270 cm) apart in November. On about April 1 the trees should be cut back to 4 ft (120 cm) above soil level and all lateral shoots pinched back to 9 in (22 cm) from the main stem. In mid-July the laterals should be shortened again, to 6 in (15 cm), and the following April the leader shortened by about one-third of the past season's wood. Then, in July prune back the laterals again to 6 in (15 cm) and in this way the tree will concentrate on making fruit buds rather than wood.

To form the fan-shaped tree, which may be planted in the open and trained against strong wires or against a wall, cut back the leader to an upwards bud and on the lower portion of the stem, about 10 in (25 cm) above the scion, to two buds, one on either side of the stem. Make a nick in the bark above the buds to persuade them to 'break'. When the two buds have made 18 in

(45 cm) of growth, cut the leader back to just above the topmost shoot. Then tie two shoots to canes at an angle of 45°. At the end of summer, cut back these side arms to a bud about 9 in (22 cm) from the base; then, during next summer allow laterals on the upper part of the two arms to grow on. Cut back the arms to the laterals furthest from the base. The framework will then be established.

The only pruning necessary will be to pinch back the newly formed shoots when they have formed seven or eight leaves. Do this in early July and tie the shoots in to prevent wind damage.

Root pruning

Often fan trees, and, indeed, all types of plum tree, begin to form suckers. These are shoots that arise from the roots below the scion and they must be removed. Uncover the roots around the stem and, taking care not to damage the scion, cut away the suckers with a sharp knife before covering the roots again and treading firm.

At the same time, root pruning may be done. This is the best way of restricting growth with plums, for there will be no 'bleeding'. It is usually fan-trained trees growing against a wall that are root-pruned. Scrape away the soil to a distance of 4–5 ft (120–150 cm) from the wall to uncover the roots and cut them back to about 3 ft (1 m) of the stem. This will encourage more fibrous roots to form. Scatter peat around the roots before replacing the soil and tread firmly. Then give the roots a good soaking.

The choice of rootstocks is not large. Dwarf trees are grown on Common plum or Brompton stock and in the United States on sand cherry, Nanking cherry and St Julian A plum. Standards are grown on the Myrobolan stock. This is mostly used for heavy-bearing orchard trees. Owing to their 'gumming', plums are budded, as with roses, and not grafted.

Plums enjoy best a heavy loam. They will grow well in a limestone soil provided there is plenty of humus present, but they require a moisture-retentive soil and one that receives plenty of nitrogen, preferably of an organic nature. In light soils, work in plenty of farmyard or poultry manure, peat moss or compost. At planting time, give a handful of bone meal or superphosphate to each tree, mixed well into the soil as it is placed over the roots. The trees should also be given a liberal mulch of organic manure in spring each year, augmented by 1 oz (28 g) of sulphate of ammonia.

Harvesting and storing

Plums must be allowed to remain on the trees until fully ripe. The best test will be to remove one when it is thought to be ripe and taste it. If it is soft and juicy and the stone readily parts from the flesh, it is ripe. Most plums will store for several weeks in a dry, airy room if removed from the plant with their stalks and placed in cotton in trays.

Pollination

As with apples and pears, some thought must be given to pollination.

The flowering time of plums is from eighteen to twenty-one days, so that the flowering period of many plums will overlap. Only the very early and very late do not overlap, for plums are in bloom for only ten

Plums bear on both the old and new wood, hence they crop heavily. A number of plum types exist, including varieties from abroad and the native kinds.

Opposite: All of the 'Gage' plums are prized for their fruits. This is Mirabelle Gage.

days, and not until the early plums have finished do the late ones come into bloom.

While some plums do not require cross-pollination, even these will probably bear more abundantly if another plum variety is in bloom nearby. One point to keep in mind is that American plums do not pollinate European or Japanese varieties, nor do European or Japanese varieties pollinate each other.

Varieties

DeMontfort Old European plum of high quality prized by fanciers. Dark purple, round fruit of medium size with sweet, juicy flesh. Ripens in late August in Northeast.

Early Transparent Gage European plum that makes a dwarf tree and sets a heavy crop with its own pollen. The skin is so thin as to show the stone and has an apricot flavor when fully ripe. Excellent for the home garden because it ripens over several weeks.

French Damson European oval-shaped plum, large and tart, ripening in midsummer. The Damson is famous for preserves and jams.

Golden Transparent Gage Similar to Early Transparent, though ripening later. The bright yellow fruit, speckled red, has a peach-like flavour.

Green Gage One of the most famous of European plums. With another European variety blooming at the same time, it crops heavily. Its greenish-yellow fruit is juicy and sweet, and unsurpassed in flavor. It forms a neat, compact tree. Ripens mid-season.

Ozark Premier Japanese plum popular in the Midwest. Large, bright red fruits ripen in midsummer.

Santa Rosa Japanese plum, large and dark red-purple in color. High quality. Ripens midsummer on. Trees grow large except in dwarf sizes.

Shiro This golden plum, a Japanese variety, begins to ripen in midsummer. Forms a low tree.

Stanley European prune type for dessert or preserving. Dark blue fruit with heavy bloom. Very productive. Ripens mid-season.

Underwood An American plum of exceptional hardiness, suitable for colder states and into Canada. Red-purple fruit in midsummer.

Superior Japanese plum acts as pollinator for other Japanese varieties. Red fruits ripen in midsummer.

Yellow Egg European plum, oval with yellow skin and flesh. Sweet and juicy and self-pollinating.

Green Gages make delicious eating if removed when just ripe.

25

Wild plums native to America

There are, of course, species of the plum family that are native to the North American continent. In fact, the genus *Prunus*, which encompasses both the plums and cherries, has over 200 different species of trees and shrubs widely distributed through the North American Temperate Zone – and a few even extend into the tropics.

The American Plum, *Prunus americana*, is a relatively small tree, about 20 to 35 ft (6–10 m) high. It bears ill-smelling flowers, with round, red fruits which are about 1 in (2·5 cm) in diameter. The flesh is tart and yellow.

The Mexican Plum, *Prunus mexicana*, bears dark, purple-red fruits about 1½ in (4 cm) long, with thick and sweet flesh. It is a taller-growing tree than the American Plum.

Much further north, the Canadian Plum, *Prunus nigra*, displays white flowers, with yellow-fleshed, orange-red plums just over 1 in (2·5 cm) long. It is a tree with distinctive bark that is gray-brown and peels off in layers.

Native to the West Coast is the Klamath Plum, *Prunus subcordata*. Growing to 25 ft (7·5 m) high, it produces tart, dark-red or occasionally yellow fruits about 1 in (2·5 cm) long.

The Flatwoods Plum, *Prunus umbellata*, which heralds from the Southern states, produces tart plums that are purplish-black in color although they are on occasion yellow.

Coming from around the New England area is the Allegheny Plum, *Prunus alleghaniensis*. It somewhat resembles the Flatwoods Plum, but the slightly larger leaves are narrower. Globular plums are produced, with dark reddish-purple skins and yellow flesh. The Allegheny Plum is a smallish tree, with bark that is scaly and dark brown.

From the lower Ohio and lower Mississippi valleys come the Wildgoose Plum,

Damson plums are untroubled by cold winds or frosts and so may be planted as a windbreak.

Prunus munsoniana, with palatable plums of good quality. The red fruits are just under an inch (2·5 cm) in length.

The Hortulan Plum, *Prunus hortulana*, with leaves 4–6 in (10–15 cm) long and slender orange stems, produces red, or occasionally yellow, fruits.

The Chickasaw Plum, *Prunus angustifolio*, is an interesting plum, originally a native of the South Atlantic and Gulf states. However, it is now naturalized throughout many areas, where it often forms impenetrable thickets in old fields and waste areas. Numerous horticultural varieties have been developed from the Chickasaw Plum for use in southern orchards, but, unfortunately, the fruits are seldom of a really good quality.

Originating from southeastern Texas is the Larissa Plum, *Prunus tenuifolia*. The fruits have very thin flesh.

5 Cherries

Though always in demand for dessert and culinary use, being the first of the fruits to ripen, sweet cherries are now rarely planted in the amateur's garden. They do well only as standard or half-standard trees, on which they take about ten years to bear a prolific crop. Again, there are pollination difficulties, for only cherries of certain groups will pollinate each other and several must be planted together for best results. A standard cherry needs ample space to develop and in a small garden several of the more compact apples, occupying the same amount of ground, will be a better proposition. Nor are most cherries, notably sweet varieties, as cold-hardy as apples. Birds, too, are always troublesome, for even where the fruits have set well, birds can take half the crop. But early cherries, sweet or sour, are always appreciated and where space permits, two or three varieties may be planted together. These two or three varieties might be placed in a shrub border if bush cherry varieties are ordered. Bush cherries are hybrids from an American species (*Prunus bessyi*) that are found from Manitoba to Kansas, and only grow 4–6 ft (1·22–1·83 m) tall. The bushes are of such a size that nylon netting can readily be thrown over them to protect the fruits from birds. Bush cherries are very hardy and can be grown in regions too frigid for most standard cherries. Bush cherries do require pollination from another bush cherry variety, so plant two or more different varieties.

Cherry trees do well in a variety of soils so long as they are well drained. They can not tolerate wet soil. Since growth is started so early in spring, and if there is any choice in the matter, sandy loams might be preferable because they warm faster. Avoid sites where the flowers can be injured by late frosts. Cherries do not require excessive fertilizing, although if the leaf color is washed out and pale green, it may be a sign that the tree needs feeding.

Planting of cherries is done in the fall. Take care not to damage the bark, for that would permit bacterial canker or silver leaf disease to enter at the wound. If planting in grass, first remove a circle of 2 ft (60 cm) diameter, and if planting standards, allow

Cherries are best grown as standards, and will bear well in a limestone soil. They take several years before bearing heavily, and they need suitable pollinators.

Morello cherries are hardy and may be grown as a windbreak or against a north wall in the fan-trained form. Most home gardeners, however, grow them as regular standard trees. The dark sour cherries are later than Montmorency.

at least 20 ft (6 m) between them. For a fan tree, provide a 16 ft (480 cm) frame of horizontally fixed wires. Plant bush cherries about 3–4 ft (90·5–120 cm) apart.

Pruning

Follow much the same pruning procedure as for plums. Fan trees are formed in the same way. Afterwards, pinch back the side shoots to about six leaves early in July; in September, pinch back to four buds. If the leader shoots are making excessive growth, bend them down as far as possible and tie in, releasing them after twelve months. Root pruning may also be done as for plums.

With standards, cut the leader shoots back to half way in April, at the same time removing any dead wood but nothing more. Eventually, cherry branches that become too tall or are outgrowing the side branches can be headed back as necessary.

Standard cherry trees are budded on two rootstocks, mazzard (*Prunus avium*) and mahaleb (*P. mahaleb*). Mazzard rootstocks are preferred for sweet cherries, although it may take the tree longer to come into bearing. Work is continuing to find suitable dwarfing understock for cherries that would limit the size of the trees and bring the trees into bearing earlier. A promising development is the genetic dwarfing of rootstocks obtained from crossing *Prunus avium* and *P. cerasus*.

Pollinating

Cherries have a flowering period of eighteen to twenty days, twice that of plums, and except for the very earliest and latest, they overlap. Yet this plays little or no part in their pollination and only certain groups will prove fertile with each other.

One way to surmount the pollination problem is to plant the true dwarf variety North Star, which will pollinate itself. Another sour cherry, Montmorency, is also self-pollinating, as is Meteor, another natural dwarf.

There is no sweet cherry that is self-pollinating. Most catalogs give pollinating information for the cherries they list. Help can also be obtained from the fruit specialists at state agricultural experiment stations or county extension associations (listed in the telephone book under the county government). Good pollinators for most sweet cherry varieties are Merton Bigarreau (but will not pollinate Windsor, Van and Venus), Sam and Van.

Varieties

Black Beauty A bush cherry with very glossy maroon-red fruits for eating fresh or using for pies and preserves.

Brooks A bush cherry with red fruits nearly as large as standard varieties. All bush cherries are very hardy.

Emperor Francis Early-blooming sweet cherry with large, high quality fruits. The dark red fruits ripen in midseason.

Golden Bush This bush cherry has attractive yellow fruits. Bush cherries all bear in early summer.

Jubilee A variety from California that is replacing Bing. Sweet black cherries ripen in midseason.

Merton Bigarreau A sweet cherry tree too large for most backyard orchards. A very productive variety, the large, dark red fruits ripening in midseason.

Meteor Semi-dwarf tree with tart, bright red fruits. Tree remains at 8–10 ft (2·45–3 m), making it useful in small gardens. Also self-pollinating.

Napoleon Also called Royal Anne. Old sweet cherry variety with yellow fruits with a red cheek or blush. Use Black Tartarian, Van or Vista to pollinate the flowers. Moderately hardy.

North Star A naturally dwarf variety that remains 6–7 ft (1·80–2·14 m) in height. The early, bright red fruits are excellent for pies. Very hardy.

Royal Duke All Duke varieties are hybrids between sweet and sour cherries. This variety has red cherries which are considered quite sweet. Another variety must be planted for cross-pollination.

Cherry trees have a flowering period twice as long as the flowering period of plums.

6 Apricots, peaches and nectarines

These are plants of the East, able to survive a cold winter but requiring a long, dry summer to ripen the fruit and the wood, without which they will bear little fruit the following year. Both apricots and peaches are good fruit crops for backyard gardens. The trees are available as both standards and dwarfs, and even the standards can be kept in bounds by pruning. There are a few peach varieties that can be grown in tubs. Most apricots and peaches are self-pollinating.

Apricots

Apricots are very tolerant of heat. They grow well in a variety of soils but they must have good drainage. Humus-forming materials, such as compost and peat moss, can be mixed in the planting holes, especially if the soils are very sandy. After planting, cut back young trees to about 2½ ft (75 cm).

Plant in autumn. Apricots can be grown as fan-trained trees against a wall. Plant at least 18 ft (5·5 m) apart, for they make long shoots. Allow the main shoots to grow on, pinching back the side growths in summer to about 2 in (5 cm).

For non-fan-shaped trees, the usual practise is to develop a main branch, or 'leader', with the lateral branches being cut back as necessary to maintain this pyramidal form.

Though self-fertile, apricots will set a better crop if hand-fertilized. This is done by dusting each flower with a camel-hair brush as they open. Apricots flower early and if they are grown against an outside wall, it is advisable to hang muslin over the plants as soon as the blooms begin to open if a late frost threatens.

When the fruits have set and have started to swell, thin them to three in a cluster and to about 3 in (8 cm) apart as they make size, removing perhaps the center one. Allow the fruit to become fully ripe before removing it.

Apricots fruit on old and new wood. To prevent overcrowding, remove the old spurs after the plants have borne fruit on them for two years.

The plants will benefit from a mulch of strawy manure each season in early summer. Once the fruit has set, you should never allow the trees to go short of moisture at the roots.

Varieties

Alfred A hardy apricot that bears bright orange, slightly blushed fruits in late July in the Northeast. Fruits are juicy and rich in flavor.

Early Golden Orange-gold fruits of good size and with virtually fuzzless skins on vigorous trees.

Hardier apricot varieties are now available for the North. Both dwarf and standard trees exist and are well-suited to the smaller fruit gardens.

Above: Prune peaches by the replacement system.

Right: Peaches crop heavily without a pollinator.

Goldcot Large golden-yellow fruits on strong trees. Cold-hardy and tolerant of humidity in summer.

Henderson Large yellow apricots with pink blush. The tree is strong and highly productive.

Moorpark Large golden-yellow fruits with pink cheeks. Considered very hardy.

Moongold Golden fruits in late summer. Originated especially for cold climates. It requires cross-pollination. The companion variety below is recommended for this purpose.

Sungold Bears a little later than above. Plant with Moongold for pollination.

Peaches

Outdoors, peaches are grown as standards or fan-trained trees against a wall; in pots on a terrace or verandah; or as dwarf trees, like apples, when they will come into fruit two years after planting. Plant in fall or early spring, allowing just over 18 ft (5 m) for fan trees and just under 6 ft (2 m) for dwarfs. They require a well-drained soil containing organic matter, a sandy loam being preferred. Peaches are budded onto seedling peaches or special dwarf stocks, and when planting, make sure that the union is above soil level. Tread in the roots firmly and water well if the soil is dry. Each year, in May, give a liberal mulch of strawy manure to conserve moisture.

Reliance Medium-sized yellow fruits, early ripening, recommended for very cold climates.

Sun Haven Bright red peaches, medium to large in size, and nearly fuzzless. Very early to ripen, about 10 days before Red Haven.

White Champion Old variety of fine quality with white flesh that ripens in midsummer. Fruits large and tree vigorous.

Nectarine

This is a smooth-skinned peach and requires similar culture in every way, plenty of sunshine to ripen its wood, and in spring a thick mulch to conserve moisture – without which the fruits will not swell to a good size.

Varieties

Nectacrest Good-sized, fine-flavored fruits with white flesh in early fall.

Nectarina A genetic dwarf like Flory and Bonanza peaches, suitable for tubs.

Mericrest A very hardy nectarine ripening in midsummer.

Pruning

At the beginning, give dwarf trees the same treatment as in the renewal system for apples, i.e. shoots that have borne fruit are grown on until they are 18 in (45 cm) long. Do the same for fan trees. Fasten them to the wall and pinch the tips back to a wood bud. This will produce the wood that will bear next year's crop. The wood buds are small and pointed, the blossom buds round and fat.

Pruning of established trees consists of, in early spring, cutting back the leaders to about one-third and, in early June, pinching back the side shoots to about 2 in (5 cm), to a single wood bud at the base. This is grown on as replacement for next season's crop. Those shoots that have fruited are removed at the end of summer. This continuous formation of replacement shoots on which the crop is carried will keep the trees free from old wood, which often causes 'gumming' when removed.

Peaches are self-fertile and need no pollinator, but a heavier set of fruit will be obtained if the open flowers, when dry, are pollinated with a camel-hair brush, especially those in a greenhouse.

Do not thin the fruit until after 'the June drop'. This is a natural falling of the fruits when about the size of fully grown cherries. There should be about 5 in (12 cm) between the fruits left to mature.

The fruit ripens from the end of July until early October, depending on variety. To determine the ripeness, place a hand beneath a fruit and lift gently upwards: it should come away easily with its stalk. Or gently press the base of a fruit: if ripe, it will be slightly soft. Ripe fruits can be kept in the refrigerator for a few days.

Varieties

Bonanza A dwarf peach that does quite well for a time in tubs. Large, yellow, freestone fruits.

Crawford An old variety whose red-tinted fruits ripen in late September in northern New York.

Elberta Famous variety with large, yellow, freestone fruits. Hardy, with fruit ripening in fall.

Flory A naturally dwarf Chinese peach with large, decorative foliage and small white-fleshed peaches in fall.

Golden Jubilee Large, yellow, freestone peaches of excellent quality in midsummer.

Red Haven Large, red peaches nearly fuzzless, of medium size. Early ripening.

Nectarines are smooth-skinned peaches that need similar culture.

7 Grapes

There is no other crop for the home fruit garden that requires the skill and dedication demanded by proper grape culture.

Where space is a problem, there is the grape arbor, a structure that was once a part of every backyard and supplied fruits and summer shelter. Or a row of grapes can be grown alongside a vegetable garden, the vines being trained on wires between posts. They can also be grown horizontally against a wall or fence. European grape varieties are sometimes grown on posts, planted 4 ft (120 cm) apart.

There are three kinds of grape vines grown in North America, each group having many named hybrids and varieties. The European grape (*Vitis vinifera*), the basis of grape culture in Britain and Europe, requires mild climates and is grown in California and a few other Western regions. In the South the native Muscadine grape (*Vitis rotundifolia*) is grown. In the North where grapes are grown, the varieties are derived from the native fox grape (*V. labrusca*) crossed with European varieties.

Though grape vines require an open, sunny situation to ripen, they are hardier to cold than imagined.

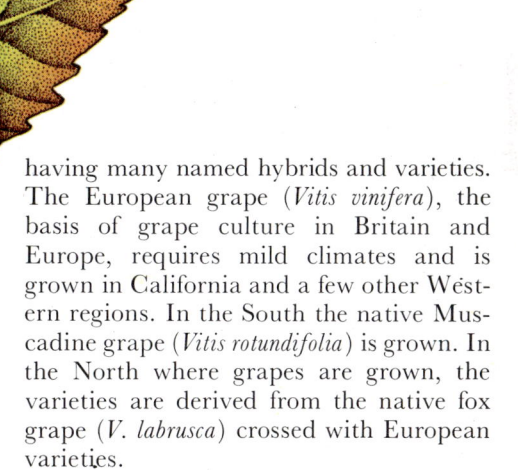

Planting

The latest information on culture, training and varieties for each region can be obtained from state agricultural experiment stations and county extension agents. The vines require a sunny site that is not

Grapes are usually planted outside, but grow well in a cold or slightly warm greenhouse, trained over the roof.

prone to late frosts in spring that can damage the flower buds. The soil should be well-drained, deeply prepared and rich in humus. A sandy loam is best, but most soils are adequate. Add compost, peat moss or rotted manure and about 10 lbs (4·50 kilograms) of superphosphate to each row of 25 ft (7·63 m). Plant in fall or early spring, spacing the vines from 6–8 ft (180–240 cm) apart. Cut back to two buds.

Training American Grapes

Unless grown over an arbor where pruning is reduced to thinning out older woody canes every few years, vines are trained to the four-cane Kniffen System, both commercially and in the home garden. The System can be used for European varieties, but they are usually trained somewhat differently (see below).

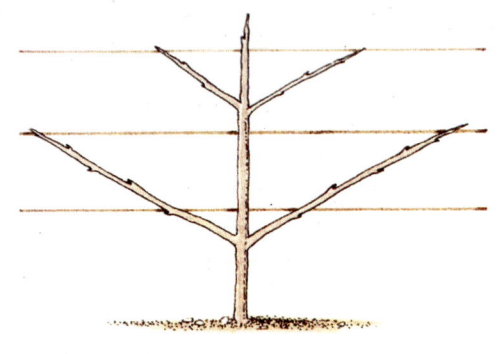

4*above*: A grape vine may be planted against a trellis in a sunny place. Tie in stems as they make growth.

For the System, strong posts are set every 10 ft (300 cm) and strung with two rows of wire, the bottom 30 in (75 cm) from the ground, the second about 36 in (90·5 cm) above it. The vine is kept to a single stem with two canes trained along the wires in each direction (four canes in all). Since grapes are borne on shoots from one-year canes, the annual pruning during winter dormancy involves removing excess growth so the vine retains its fruiting vigor but does not overproduce. There are other Systems; the Umbrella Kniffen System is also popular. Southern grape varieties are grown on arbors and are only pruned as needed to restrain growth.

Pruning European grapes

Pruning calls for some thought. A shoot will grow 20 ft (6 m) in a single season, and every eye along the entire length is capable of bearing a shoot that will produce one or more bunches of grapes. In addition, a vine is able to bear fruit on the older wood, though this would prove too much for its constitution. If new shoots are encouraged, the eyes on the old wood will not be sufficiently vigorous to bear fruit, and the fruit on the new wood will be better.

There are two main methods of pruning, the long rod system and the spur system.

The long rod system This name applies when one or two new shoots or rods are allowed to grow on and all other growth is restricted.

With vines, pruning is done in the depths of winter, the first days of January, before the sap begins to rise, being most suitable. For greenhouse plants, allow the vine to form stems or rods; train these as far apart as possible and tie in to wires stretched across the roof. The stems will grow 20 ft (6 m) or more their first year. In early winter, cut the weaker stem back to two buds near the base. On the other, stronger stem will be borne the next season's crop, and the stronger stem from its two buds will be grown on to produce the crop for the season

By the long-rod system, one or two shoots only are grown on and other growth is restricted.

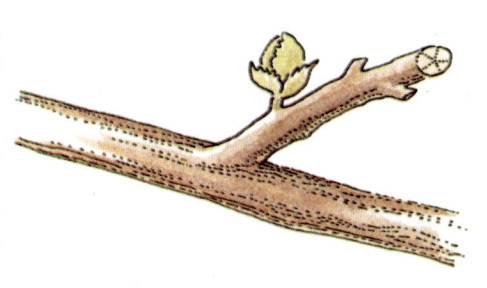

From these stems, select alternate buds on either side of the stems to produce short laterals.

after that. To prevent the formation of too much foliage, pinch back all laterals to two buds – one to bear the fruit, the other the foliage, which should be stopped at two leaves. Do this pinching back in summer over several weeks so as not to check the plant too drastically.

For vines in the open, growing vertically, follow the single rod and spur system, retaining the strongest shoot of two basal buds to bear fruit. Then, after fruiting, cut back to a single eye or bud to produce next year's rod, or stem.

The spur system From the stem that has grown away unchecked, select alternate buds on each side of the stem to produce short laterals. These bear fruit and should be stopped one leaf beyond. Then cut back each shoot to two buds in winter, one of which will form the grapes, the other the foliage. This will build up a system of spurs. Stop fruit-bearing laterals at the first joint after the bunch has formed, and pinch back non-fruiting laterals to 2 in (5 cm).

Vines growing horizontally against a wall should receive the same treatment as espalier pears. Cut back to the lower three buds in winter, the upper forming the extension shoot while the lower buds, one on either side of the stem, will form the lower arms. Train them first at an angle of 45°, tying them to canes, then gradually bring them to the horizontal position. The following year, cut back the extension shoot again to three buds, the two lower ones facing in opposite directions to form the next pair of arms, about 16 in (40 cm) above the lower pair and so on until the vine reaches the required height. Each arm or stem should be treated the same as for the spur system.

When the fruit has set it must be decided how many bunches the vines can mature. This depends upon age. Probably the stems will carry ten bunches in their second year, twice that number next year and so on. Should there be overcrowding, nip out a few grapes with pointed scissors, as well as any damaged fruits.

Varieties

American

Buffalo Blue-black early grape.

Concord Blue, midseason grape, famous for juice and jelly.

Golden Muscat Large, golden grape clusters. Late.

Himrod Seedless Golden-yellow grapes of medium size. Early.

Interlaken Seedless Amber grapes on hardy vines that rival Thompson Seedless. Very early.

Ontario White grape. Disease-resistant vines. Very early.

European

Cardinal Dark red grapes. Early.

Emperor Purple-red grapes. Late.

Muscat of Alexandria Green fruits for fresh and raisin use. Late midseason.

Southern

Burgaw Reddish-black grapes. Midseason. Self-pollinating.

Scuppernong Red-tinted green grapes. Early.

Tarheel Black grapes. Self-pollinating. Midseason.

Below: White and yellow grapes have a distinct flavor. They are usually hardier than the black varieties.

Above: Grapes growing against a wall.

Right: The Black Hamburgh grape is a famous European variety that is still grown to some extent in greenhouses. The fruit possesses a rich muscat flavor.

37

8 Figs

The fig is hardier than is generally believed. Though a native of the Near East, it crops well and will ripen its fruit almost anywhere in an average summer. In the East and in the warmer parts of the USA, it bears two to three crops a year, being continuously in bearing.

Figs do well close to the sea where the salt-laden atmosphere and sea mists give protection from frost. They prefer an average garden soil that retains moisture and is slightly acid. Avoid too much fertilizer, for figs make plenty of leaf without it. They need a sparse diet and this means restricting the roots so that they cannot go far in search of food.

Planting

Obtain pot-grown plants and either plant the vine in the pot, burying it below soil level, or remove from the pot with the soil ball intact, and plant over a layer of stones. These should be rammed well down to make a solid base after the soil has been removed to a depth of 18 in (45 cm). If you are planting the figs against a wall, which is a good site for them, place pieces of slate on the other three sides of a hole made 18 in (45 cm) wide, to restrict the roots still further. Then when planting the soil ball, make the soil around it as compact as possible and water in.

Growing figs in tubs is a common practice in much of the North. The tubs act to restrict root growth and make it easier to move the plants into more sheltered areas over winter. Or plants are wrapped in straw and burlap which serves as protection against freezing temperatures.

Figs are planted in spring and require copious amounts of water through summer. They should also be given a thick mulch in May each year. They grow well in the horizontal form planted against a west wall, leaving a south-facing wall either for peaches or for pears.

Figs ripen well when planted against a warm wall.

Pruning

The fruit is carried on the previous year's wood. The replacement shoot is stopped at the fourth leaf, at the end of July – not before, as the fruits expected to manure the following summer will form too quickly at the expense of new wood. Yet if the shoot is not stopped, the tiny figs will lack nourishment, turn yellow and fall off.

The fruits form at the leaf axils the previous year and begin to swell in spring. If the shoots are pinched back late in July, new fruits will form at the axil of each leaf and will be next year's crop. If the tree begins to make too much wood, some of that which carried the previous season's fruit should be thinned.

Figs in greenhouses, growing in gentle heat, will bear two crops yearly. The fruits formed the previous year will swell early in spring and be ripe by early summer, then those formed in spring will mature by late

September. The shoots formed in the last weeks of summer will bear next spring's crop.

Propagation is a simple matter. It is either by cuttings or by suckers. By the former method a well-ripened shoot 8 in (20 cm) long should be removed in January. The base is dipped in hormone powder to encourage rapid rooting, before being inserted in a small pot containing a gritty compost. It should be placed over a radiator or in a propagating unit, for bottom heat is necessary; it will root in three months. Re-pot into a large pot before placing outdoors in May, in a sunny position to ripen the wood. Plant it in its permanent place the following spring. Or the plants may be moved to larger pots in which they will fruit. They should be 6 ft (180 cm) apart, for they will soon reach that height and will grow to the same width.

The method by which plants are grown on from suckers is the easier way. These should be detached with their roots and grown on in pots.

To harvest figs, remove them before they split but not much before. Place them in trays lined with cotton. They may be kept for several months in a frost-free room.

Varieties

Brown Turkey The best all-round hardy fig, good under glass and outdoors, bearing heavy crops of large purple-brown fruits of excellent flavor.

Brunswick Good under glass, it needs a sheltered, sunny position outdoors. The large green figs have white flesh.

Plant in a tub, or remove with soil ball intact and restrict roots by planting over a layer of stones.

Fruits form in the leaf axils the previous year. Pinch back the shoots in July to encourage new fruits to form.

9 Raspberries

A cane fruit to follow strawberries as the chief soft fruit of summer with everbearing types producing fall harvests, too. It freezes well and with its unique flavor makes excellent preserves. The plants flower later than strawberries and are rarely troubled by frost.

Raspberries require an open sunny situation. To enable the canes to receive the full amount of sunshine, plant the rows north to south. A plantation will be permanent, although raspberries fruit on the previous

Above: Raspberries ripen after strawberries, fruiting on the previous year's canes.

Left: Raspberries bear well in a humus-laden soil if not planted too deep.

year's canes and it is necessary to provide the plants with a moderately fertile soil in order to enable them to make plenty of growth.

Raspberry plants also need humus in order to retain summer moisture, without which there will be few new canes and the fruits will be hard and seedy.

Preparing the ground

Dig in all the humus possible, including some peat moss together with manure or rotted compost. Use large amounts if the soil is of a sandy nature. At planting time, rake in 1 oz of sulfate of potash per yd (30 g per m) of row, or of wood ash that has been stored under cover.

It is important to plant into clean ground, for it will be difficult to clean after planting without damaging the roots, as this fruit is surface-rooting. Rather than hoe too near the plants, give a mulch of compost and rotted straw in early June each year. This will suppress weeds and preserve moisture in the soil.

Planting

Plant the canes in spring in the North so that they are established before the frosts, although planting can be done at any time until mid-March if the soil is in a friable condition. If not, dig a trench and spread out the roots before covering them with soil until planting can take place. As with all fruits, purchase from a reliable grower who offers virus-free stock, very important with raspberries.

Plant the canes 24–30 in (60–75 cm) apart, the black and purple varieties needing slightly wider spacing; allow 4 ft (120 cm) between the rows. Do not plant too deeply, for this is the cause of failure of many plantations. Just cover the roots and tread in the soil over them. Then after a few days, cut back the canes to 6 in (15 cm) above ground level. There will be no fruit the first summer, though the autumn-fruiting kinds will bear a crop. This cutting back will cause the buds at the base of the canes to produce new canes on which will be borne next year's crop.

As the canes make growth, tie them to wires stretched along the rows at intervals of 18 in (45 cm). This will prevent the canes being broken by winds. At the end of summer, remove the tips of the canes, which will then have grown about 6 ft (180 cm) tall. After fruiting, cut out the old canes to about 3 in (7 cm) above ground and tie in the new canes for next year's crop. Burn the old canes and leave each root with six to seven new fruiting canes.

With autumn-fruiting kinds, the canes that fruited in fall can be headed back to force branching and a bigger crop on the same canes in early summer. The new fall crop is borne on canes which are produced that summer. In all other respects, the culture is the same for them.

The fruit ripens quickly, and if the weather is warm it may need picking twice daily so that it will not get too ripe and become 'mushy'.

To propagate, lift a root or two in spring or fall and separate the canes, holding them near the base and pulling them away with the roots. Re-plant as soon as possible so that the roots do not dry out, treating them as described.

Varieties

Allen Black fruits, large and glossy, firm and juicy. Begin to ripen in early July in the

When planting raspberries in rows, fasten canes to wires, cut back to 6 in (15 cm) above ground after fruiting. New canes will fruit next year.

Northeast. The fruits tend to ripen at about the same time, an advantage for commercial growers and perhaps for some home fruit growers, too.

Black Hawk Black raspberries, large and sweet. Very productive with berries ripening for several weeks.

Bristol Black berries, large, glossy, of high quality. Midseason ripening.

Clyde A purple-fruited variety developed by the New York Experimental Station at Geneva, New York. A late variety, the fruits start to ripen in mid-July.

Fall Gold Large, golden-yellow berries, appearing in early July and again in the fall until frosts arrive. Very vigorous.

Fall Red Everbearing, the first red berries appearing about July 1, the fall crop starting in mid-August and continuing until frosts arrive.

An early variety which is widely grown in Europe, where it produces heavy crops.

Early to ripen, Malling Promise bears heavy crops.

Heritage Everbearing, the red fruits appearing early and again about September 1.

Newburgh An older variety that tends to be virus-resistant. A good midseason bearer.

Sentry A high-quality red raspberry from the University of Maryland and recommended for the Middle Atlantic region. Described as early-midseason.

September Everbearer with medium-sized red fruits, first ripening the end of June in much of the Northeast, with the fall crop ripening the beginning of September. Vigorous, highly tolerant of dry conditions and always bears well.

Sodus A purple-fruited variety popular in the Midwest.

Taylor Large-fruited red berries of exceptionally high quality, these are vigorous, hardy plants with sturdy, upright canes. They ripen midseason, continuing for about three weeks.

10 Blackberries

Blackberries rarely appear in the market these days as the berries are too fragile for shipping. The commercial production goes into jams and jellies. So the only way to savor these sun-ripened, juicy berries at their peak of perfection is to grow them in the home garden. Although blackberries are not as hardy as raspberries and can be damaged by long periods of below-zero winter weather as well as late spring freezes, they do well over much of the country. A few plants can be very productive. The berries freeze well and make excellent tarts and preserves.

There are various ways of growing the plants. They can be grown along a fence or wall, or used as a hedge, possibly to divide one part of the garden from another, with a central archway for access. Or plant in rows and train the stems along wires held in place by strong stakes at intervals of 8 ft (240 cm). Plant in early spring 8 ft (240 cm) apart in the rows and allow 5 ft (150 cm) between the rows. Where possible, plant thornless varieties, which are easier to tie in and to pick the fruit from. Set the roots only 3–4 in (7–10 cm) deep.

Another method is to grow them up 10 ft (3 m) poles, or posts driven well into the ground with 8 ft (240 cm) above ground. Tie in the shoots as they grow, and when they have made too much old wood, cut away the ties and lay all the shoots on the ground. Then cut the older wood and tie in against the new shoots. In this way, the plants will be kept healthy for years. The time to do this is in fall or early spring; at this time any old or dead wood is removed from plants grown as a hedge or in rows.

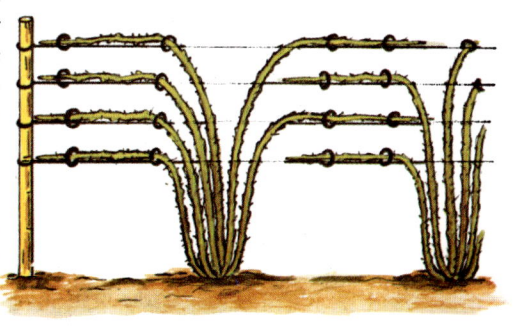

Above: Where growing on wires, space wires 18 in (45 cm) apart, using strong stakes to support them. Plant blackberries 8 ft (240 cm) apart in the rows.

Left: Blackberries may be grown against a trellis to serve as a hedge, or along wires or against a north wall.

Preparation of the soil

The plants require plenty of humus to retain moisture and produce large and juicy fruits. Give the ground some peat moss and whatever humus is available, such as garden compost or old manure. The plants will also benefit from a yearly mulch of lawn mowings or compost, to conserve soil moisture. In spring 28 g (1 oz) of sulfate of potash should be scattered on the surface around each plant. Or apply a sprinkling of 5–10–5 complete fertilizer. This will improve the quality of fruit. Blackberries will benefit from an occasional watering during wet weather of dilute liquid manure – as indeed will all soft fruits. This should be given from July until September and will not only enhance the quality of fruit but will also increase cane growth.

After planting, which should be done in spring in the North, in fall or winter in the South and other mild climates, if possible, cut back the canes to 6 in (15 cm) above soil level. New canes will appear in spring and these should be tied to wires horizontally, or vertically if they are growing against poles. Blackberries bear fruit on second-year canes.

Propagation

Named varieties are propagated by rooting the tips of the branches or canes. They are bent down from the wires in July and the ends inserted into the soil to a depth of about 3 in (7 cm). Tread firmly and keep moist. By November they will have rooted and may then be severed from the parent plant with about 6 in (15 cm) of cane attached. They should then be moved to their fruiting quarters and the parent cane should be tied in again. Nothing could be easier.

Blackberries can be grown against poles in the same way as rambler roses, tying in the long shoots.

Boysen or **Boysenberry** Large mulberry-colored fruits, the result of a cross between a dewberry and loganberry. The plants are vines, which are growing vigorously, and they need support. They are best in the milder climates, such as the South and Pacific Coast. There is a thornless form of boysenberry available.

Darrow Probably the best variety for most Northern regions. Bears a little later than Bailey.

Varieties

Bailey Large black berries that begin ripening in early summer.

Snyder Rust-resistant variety.

Lucretia Lucretia is a dewberry which has fruits that are larger and milder-flavoured than those of the blackberry.

Thornfree An origination of the US Dept. of Agriculture. Black fruits appear later than Darrow. Its advantage is its lack of thorns. Smoothstem is similar, but more upright growing and a week or so later than Thornfree in ripening.

Other members of the blackberry tribe

There are, of course, many other members of the blackberry tribe, including the loganberry, which is discussed on the following page. Some of these have their ancestry in America. For instance, the Parsley-leaved blackberry was formerly known as the American blackberry, although it is not actually of American origination. It is a variety of one of the British native wild species and initially was found growing wild in the county of Surrey. It was probably the species *Rubus fruticosus*, which is notable for its elegantly cut leaves and large, sweet, juicy berries. When ripe, these are distinctively black.

Another berry-bearing bramble is the species called the Himalaya berry, which does not have any connection with Himalaya but is said to have originated in America. It is exceedingly rampant, making shoots 8 to 10 ft (2·5 to 3 m) long in a single season. When established it is a very heavy cropper.

The Kugo Acre berry is supposed to be a variety of the American blackberry, bearing long berries which are black in color when ripe. It is not so vigorous as the Himalaya berry.

The Laxtonberry is of British origin, and reputed to be a cross between the loganberry and the raspberry. The berries are large, round, and raspberry-like and they are excellent for use in either jam or jelly-making.

The Veitchberry is a hybrid between the old variety November Abundance raspberry and a blackberry, and was introduced as far back as 1902 by the firm of Messrs. James Veitch and Sons.

There are many other berried plants to be found in North America, a number of which were put to very good use by the early settlers and were subsequently cultivated in gardens.

The hybrid berries fruit in autumn and are excellent for preserves and for freezing, to use in pies during winter.

11 Loganberries

Above: Loganberries, a blackberry for mild climates.

Believed to be a red-fruiting form of the blackberry, or the result of a chance cross between a blackberry and a raspberry, the loganberry was discovered by Judge Logan at Santa Cruz and named in his honor.

Loganberries do not like cold winds and the canes are more frost-tender than either raspberries or blackberries. Hence they are grown only in California and the Northwest.

Provide the plants with a soil containing plenty of humus, for they fruit only on the new season's canes and as much new cane growth as possible must be produced. Farmyard manure, poultry manure and composted straw are all valuable, or dig in some peat moss and garden compost and give a handful of bone meal for each plant. In April, give the rows 1 oz per yd (30 g per m) of sulphate of ammonia during wet weather. This will increase cane growth, on which next year's fruit will be borne.

Plant any time between November and early March, 6 ft (180 cm) apart, only just covering the roots. In March, cut back the canes to 6 in (15 cm) above ground, and tie in the new canes as they grow. Like raspberries, this fruit will not bear a crop the first year. Should the cane tips have been caught by frost, remove them in spring when the plants are given a heavy mulch. During August, they will be laden with large crimson berries, which do not part from the core and so freeze and bottle well.

Propagation is by rooting the tips of the canes as for blackberries.

Loganberries can be increased quite easily by rooting the tips of the branches or canes. These shoots are bent down and the ends are inserted into the soil to a depth of about 3 in (7 cm). Firm the soil well around the tips, and keep them moist. The shoots will have rooted by November, and can be severed from the parent plant, with about 6 in (15 cm) of the cane attached. They can then be moved to their fruiting quarters.

Below: Train the canes against wires like raspberries.

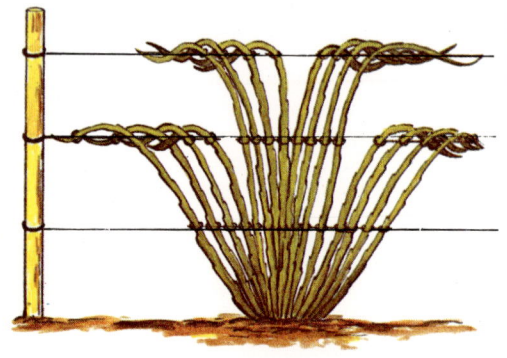

12 Gooseberries

Gooseberries are the hardiest of the soft fruits, cropping well where few other fruits would. They are troubled neither by frost nor by cold winds.

One of the hardiest of the soft fruits, the gooseberry prefers cool conditions to ripen. It does better where cool, moist conditions prevail. It crops heavily for the area of ground it occupies, and no amount of frost or cold winds will trouble it. It is one of the few soft fruits to do well in semi-shade. It may, therefore, be planted between apples and other top fruits, thus making the best use of the ground. It is also a very permanent plant and with the minimum of attention will continue to produce fruit for fifty years and more. In addition, the fruit will hang on the bushes for several weeks so that it may be picked when there is plenty of time to do so. But it should not be left until the fruits begin to crack and fall from the plants. The fruit is used for preserves, and it will freeze better than any, keeping for two years. Fresh, ripe gooseberries have no equal for flavor eaten from the plant, a treat unfortunately known to few Americans, since gooseberries are rarely grown today. Reasons for their lack of popularity are the very thorny plants and, in common with the currant, their susceptibility to white pine blister rust, of which they are an alternate host. If there are no white pines within 1000 ft, it should be safe to grow gooseberries and currants.

Gooseberries will ripen early in midsummer in the North. What is more, a

47

A well grown and carefully pruned gooseberry bush will yield fruit for many years.

pound of gooseberries can be picked in a few minutes (but wear gloves!) and the fruit does not turn mushy, however warm the weather. It is the foolproof fruit with a distinctive flavor all of its own.

Preparing the soil

Gooseberries, which fruit both on the old and new wood, bear so heavily that it is necessary to maintain a balance between the production of new wood and fruiting. The soil in which gooseberries grow needs humus to maintain moisture in summer. Without this the fruits cannot swell and will lack both weight and flavor. So dig in plenty of peat moss or garden compost, or rotted manure.

If dry conditions prevail, water the plants as often as possible, preferably in the evening, giving the roots a good soaking. All soft fruits, especially the gooseberry, require plenty of moisture for the berries to grow large and juicy. An occasional application of dilute manure water given in early summer will help the fruits to swell and increase the flavor.

Watering should commence as soon as the fruits have formed and should continue until ripe. If left until the berries have grown large, heavy watering will then cause the skins to crack, as with tomatoes.

Planting

Plant in the fall when there is no frost. But where the ground is heavy and not well-drained, early spring planting is better. Plant 4 ft (120 cm) apart in rows, with the same distance between them, for a fully grown plant will cover an area of just under a square yard (square meter).

During the first three or four years, little or no pruning is needed. Afterwards, begin to remove some of the old wood and thin out the shoots if there is overcrowding, so that the plants do not grow into each other. Those of spreading and somewhat drooping habit should have the shoots cut back to an upwards bud to counteract this tendency. Those of upright habit are cut back at an outwards bud in order to prevent overcrowding at the center.

Propagation

Gooseberry cuttings are difficult to root, for

the wood is relatively hard. Because of this, use only the new season's wood and insert as soon as possible after removing it from the plant. Cuttings are removed early September when about 6 in (15 cm) long. Remove all but the top three buds so that the plant will form a 'leg' and insert the

Gooseberries are grown on a 'leg', with the lower buds being removed before the cuttings are rooted.

Cuttings can be rooted in a cold frame or in the open ground, where they can be protected over winter by a mulch or by a plastic adaptation of the cloche.

49

Home-grown gooseberries are delicious, and are excellent for preserves and the freezer.

base in hormone powder to encourage quicker rooting. Then insert the lower 1 in (2 cm) into the soil either in trenches outdoors into which peat has been incorporated, or in a frame, the soil having been prepared in the same way. Those in trenches can be covered with cloches.

Plant the cuttings 3 in (7 cm) apart and make the soil firm around them. Water in and keep the soil comfortably moist. They should have rooted by early the following summer, but keep growing them on until October when they should be moved to their fruiting quarters and planted at the recommended spacing. They will begin to fruit the following year, but strawberries may be grown between the rows until such time as the gooseberries have made some growth.

An alternative method of propagation for gooseberries, perhaps easier than the above, is mound layering. This is the method used commercially, but it is a perfectly feasible one for the home gardener. Select one bush (or more if needed), cut back to about 6 in (15 cm) in spring. Then, in early summer, mound up soil over the entire bush, but leaving the tips of the shoots uncovered. By the next spring, the shoots covered by soil will be rooted and can be cut from the old plant and replanted. If only one or two new plants are wanted, this can be achieved by simple layering: select a branch, bend it to the ground and bury in the soil, about 1 ft (30 cm) from the tip. Fasten it securely in the soil with a U-bent wire or stone. The branch should be rooted the following year and can be cut from the parent plant.

Varieties

Fredonia Large, dark red berries in mid- to late summer. Vigorous and productive.

Pixwell Pink-red (when fully ripe) berries that hang freely from the underside of canes for better stripping.

Poorman The fruits are large and judged to be of excellent flavor.

Welcome Large, dull-red berries. The plants are reputed to be nearly thornless and are highly disease-resistant.

Growing Giant Gooseberries

Many people like to produce, either in competition or for their amusement, very large gooseberries.

These are produced by pruning each bush to several fruit-bearing shoots, feeding the bush more than normal, and thinning the berries through several stages to just a few berries.

The fruits, of course, will have to be protected from pests, especially birds, which could soon destroy the champion-sized fruits.

If bird damage is usually bad in your area, you should delay pruning the bushes until early March. By that time, there will be other berries about for the birds to attack and eat.

13 Currants

The currant, though revered in Britain and Europe, is of minor importance in the USA. The fruits (red, white, or black) are borne on bushes only 3–4 ft (90–120 cm) high that can readily be fitted into even the smallest property, but they are tart and at their best only in jelly and jam.

Probably a more important factor in the currant's lack of popularity is that the bushes are alternate hosts of the disease white pine blister rust. Although the currant bushes can survive the rust when both sides of the leaves are sprayed weekly with zineb or maneb after buds form and up to flowering, the white pines usually succumb, and many states prohibit the growing of currants to protect their white pine forests. The black currant, considered an even more effective transmitter of the rust to white pines, is virtually an outlaw and not offered by any fruit nurseries.

Those who wish to grow red- or white-fruited currants should first check with state and local authorities (state agricultural experiment stations and cooperative extension associations, the last listed under the county government in the telephone book) to find out about restrictions against currants.

Not all is bad with the currant, though. For those who can grow them, the fruits offer much for those interested in culinary arts. In addition to jellies and jams, there are sauces and syrups to be made and conserves to have with meats.

Soil requirements

The plants are very hardy and exceptionally long-lived. They will grow in most garden soils – from light (add plenty of humus to the planting holes) to medium and heavy. They will even bear well in light shade, unlike most fruits, but they should not be exposed to prevailing winds.

Planting and pruning

Fall planting is best. Set the bushes about 3–4 ft (90–120 cm) apart and cut back to about 3 in (7 cm) of their base. It is recommended that bushes be set slightly deeper than their original depth to force new shoot growth rather than allowing the bushes to grow with a single stem. No more pruning will be required until the bushes reach three years; then each autumn, all those canes which are over three years old should be removed.

The fruits begin to show color in midsummer, when they should be covered with netting to protect them from birds. Fruits for jelly possess the most pectin just before they are fully ripe. Fully ripe berries, sprinkled with sugar and wine, can be eaten fresh.

The black currant is a continental favorite.

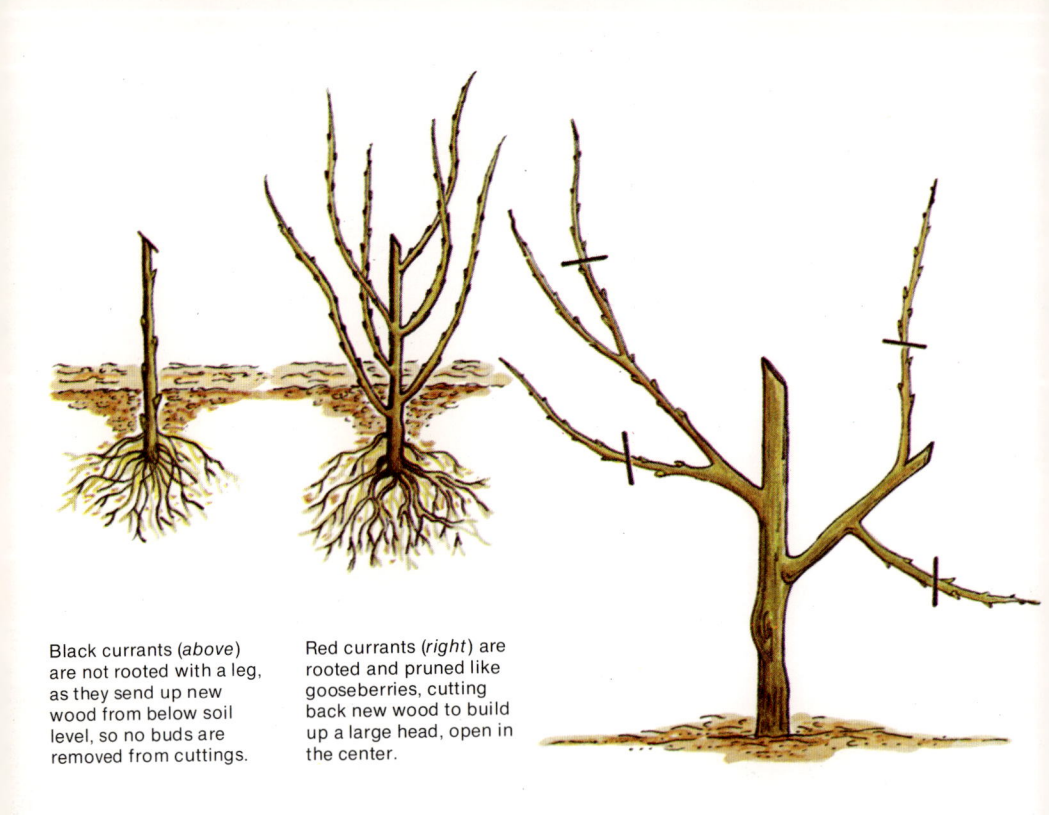

Black currants (*above*) are not rooted with a leg, as they send up new wood from below soil level, so no buds are removed from cuttings.

Red currants (*right*) are rooted and pruned like gooseberries, cutting back new wood to build up a large head, open in the center.

Training

Although white currants and red currants are usually grown as bushes, they can also be positioned against a wall. In such positions they can be formed into single, double or even triple cordons. When set against a wall it is far easier to protect them from birds than if positioned as bushes in the middle of the fruit plot. Nets can be secured to the wall and draped over the cordons.

Red or white currants can also be formed into fan-trained trees, when they are best set 6 ft (2 m) apart. Cordons can be 1 to 1½ ft (30 to 45 cm) apart. Often, these soft fruits can be advantageously positioned along walls between young wall-trained apple or pear trees. Then, after a few years when the apple and pear trees have grown, the currants can be removed.

Varieties

Minnesota 71 Large clusters of large red berries of excellent quality.

Red Lake Popular and prolific with large red berries.

White Imperial A white currant.

Wilder Large red fruits that remain in good condition on bushes after ripening if protected from birds.

Where did currants originate?

When the currant was first cultivated is difficult to say. There is no doubt that the Dutch cultivated both the red and the white currant, and that this was a long time before they became popular throughout the British Isles.

The word currant is derived from the name 'Corinth'. Currants, of course, did not originate in Corinth, which is too warm for their successful cultivation. But a variety of small grape was grown in Greece, and its likeness to the currant gave the latter its name.

The white currant is but a simple variety of the red currant, which botanically is known as *Ribes rubrum*. The black currant is a quite distinctive species, *Ribes nigrum*, and was formerly known as the Quinsy berry. It gained this name because its fruits were used to ward off, and to act as a remedy for, various infections of the throat and also for colds.

Medicinal uses of currants

The currant has for a long time been considered by herbalists to have special curative qualities.

Its uses have ranged from a cure for oral and throat ailments to strengthening gums. Also, it has been used in the treatment of fevers, especially in infants and children. Its use has even been extended to attempts at preventing miscarriages and curing anemia. It is also proclaimed to be useful against all disorders of pregnancy. And, amazingly, its use in the past also extended to a remedy for dysentery.

However, in modern-day times the currant's merit is as a useful source of vitamins especially vitamin C.

Red currants require a warm, sheltered garden. The fruit ripens July and August and should be covered with muslin to protect from birds.

The red currant is thought to be a better and more powerful laxative than the black species, although it does not seem to possess the same curative powers for the throat and mouth. According to old herbals, the red currant is said to be of value for all fevers, constipation, jaundice and all disorders of the liver. The dosage is normally one cupful of the berries twice daily. But for disorders of the liver or jaundice, a brew of the leaves is recommended. This is made by boiling the red currant leaves in water, and then taking a morning cupful of the resulting liquid.

14 Strawberries

The most popular home garden fruit, always prominent on special summer occasions, to be enjoyed in shortcake or with cream or sprinkled with wine. Strawberries freeze well and, of course, are famous for jams, preserves and sauces.

They are popular with home gardeners because they are quick to bear compared to most fruits. Everbearers (strawberry varieties that bear two crops a year) planted in early spring will yield a crop the following fall. June bearers (strawberry varieties that bear one major crop in early summer) will give a good crop the second year (they will bear the summer after planting but all flower buds are picked off to build the plant's strength for the following season).

Yet the strawberry ripens quickly, needing constant attention with its picking, and its blossom is more liable to frost damage in some regions than other fruits. The plants are more troubled by pests and diseases. Finally the fruits may be spoiled by prolonged rainy weather when ripening. Even with these disadvantages, the strawberry remains America's favorite home garden fruit and commercial production is constantly heavy.

Most home gardeners choose everbearers today, of which there are several good varieties that do well over much of the North. Everbearers perform less successfully in the South, where June bearers are usually selected. Whatever variety is ordered, make sure the plants are certified as being virus-free.

Although winter hardiness varies among varieties, the main problems are due to alternate freezing and thawing of the soil, which heaves the shallow-rooted plants out of the soil; and to injury to flower buds from late spring frosts. Avoid planting in low ground where frost can settle.

Preparing the soil

Strawberries grow best on light land; if

Strawberries are the most popular of summer fruits.

heavy, it will tend to be badly drained in winter when the roots may decay because of red stele, turning red at the center and causing the plant to die back. But light land will need plenty of humus and this may be given as peat moss, garden compost, and rotted manure. Strawberries bear better in a slightly acid soil and peat will encourage this. With it, mix in any other form of humus to bind the soil.

Clean land is essential, for the plants send out in all directions runners that take root, and it is impossible to clean round the plants later. Also, in weed-infested land the weeds deprive the plants of moisture and soon the strawberries begin to die back. If you are planting in newly turned turf land, you should treat for wireworm and grubs before planting.

Planting

Allow the ground several weeks to consolidate before planting. Before planting, rake in 1 oz per yd (30 g per m) of 5–10–5 or a similar complete fertilizer.

The Hill System or a modified version is most successful in home gardens, especially with everbearers, which form fewer runners. In this System, plants are set out 15–18 in (37–45 cm) apart in rows with about 18–24 in (45–60 cm) between rows. Keep the plants mulched, either with straw (from this use of straw the plant took its name), pine needles, leaves or, except in the South, black plastic. In winter the plants must have extra mulch applied right over the crowns to protect them from freezing temperatures and to prevent the plants from being uprooted by fluctuating soil temperatures.

The plants must be kept moist if they are to make plenty of healthy foliage and the berries are to be large and juicy. Therefore, in dry weather give plenty of water, though ample humus in the soil before planting helps retain moisture. Mid- to late summer is a good time to apply a fertilizer high in nitrogen. Any lawn fertilizer will do, especially one containing nitrogen in the urea form. Apply at the rate recommended for lawns and water in, washing any fertilizer off the foliage.

If the land is heavy and not well-drained, it will be advisable to plant on ridges or on a raised bed to allow winter rains to drain away. Also, plants on raised beds are less liable to be damaged by frost. This type of bed is made 6 in (15 cm) higher than the surrounding land and 5 ft (150 cm) across to allow for picking without treading the bed. Plant 15 in (37 cm) apart in rows 16–18 in (40–45 cm) apart.

Runners begin to form towards the end of summer, and in the Hill System are removed before they begin to root. This will enable the plants to concentrate on fruit production and in this way the plants may be productive for four or five years. A few plants may be allowed to form runners, which are removed when they have formed roots. These are used to make a new plantation each year, to take over when the original plantings begin to bear poorer-quality berries.

When planting, use a blunt-ended trowel and make the hole large enough to take all the roots and to enable them to be spread out. Only just cover the roots, with the crown of the plant at soil level. Use a garden line to make the rows, which should run north to south. Tread the plants in and do so again in spring for some may have been lifted by frost.

When the green berries have turned white, inspect them daily for they will soon turn pink and then scarlet, this taking only

Where the ground is not well-drained, plant strawberries on ridges or on a raised bed.

Plant with a blunt-edged trowel, being careful to spread out the roots before covering with soil.

a few days, or less in warm weather. Pick them with the calyx attached if possible and place in a refrigerator to cool. Then remove the green tops, sprinkle with sugar and replace until required.

Growing in tubs

Good crops can be obtained by planting in tubs or barrels used by cider and vinegar makers. They need drilling with drainage holes at the base, and also round the side at intervals of about 15 in (37 cm). Make the holes large enough to take the roots with the foliage outside the hole.

The tubs and barrels can be of any size and may be placed in a courtyard where there is no garden. They need as much sunshine as possible. First treat the tubs with wood preservative (though being of oak, they will usually be long lasting) and the iron bands with paint or a rustproof material. Then place a layer of broken-up pieces from clay pots or pebbles at the bottom, to cover the drainage holes and to permit surplus moisture to escape. Over these pieces, place some coarse compost, then fill up to within 1 in (2·5 cm) of the top with prepared loam, peat and decayed manure, mixed well together. Also, give a handful of superphosphate to each tub; twice that amount to each barrel.

Plant 6 in (15 cm) apart in a tub and put a plant in each hole in a barrel. Water from the top and, from spring, keep the plants well supplied with moisture, for they will obtain only limited amounts naturally.

Varieties

Black Beauty Large, dark red June bearer, that is a flavorful novelty for the home garden.

Geneva This is a large, high-quality berry. The plants bear well in June, through the summer and into early fall. A fine everbearer from the NY Agricultural Experiment station.

Ogallala An everbearer from the University of Nebraska. A large and productive strawberry.

Ozark Beauty Popular everbearer of fine-flavored berries to use either fresh or for freezing.

Premier An early June bearer, this old variety retains its popularity.

Sparkle June bearer, midseason to late. Attractive fruits of good flavor.

Surecrop This is a June bearer that lives up to its name. It has deep red berries of sweet flavor.

Where did strawberries originate?

Unquestionably, the strawberry is one of the most delicious of our hardy fruits. It is also one of the most adaptable – being used in jams, pies and perhaps best of all being eaten on its own with cream.

In its wild state it can be found in many parts of the world, on hedge banks and in woods. It is especially abundant in northern Europe. In fact, the wild strawberry is often appreciated more than the cultivated

If there is no ground available, heavy crops may be obtained from strawberries grown in barrels or tubs. Be sure to prepare the soil well before planting.

Everbearing strawberries provide a second harvest beginning in midsummer.

one. Its taste is less watery than many modern-day varieties.

As far back as the thirteenth century in Britain mention was made of them. They were mentioned in the Household Roll of the Countess of Leicester. And by the time of King Henry VIII, the fruit was valued at fourpence a bushel – a good sum of money for those days.

The strawberries grown at that time were the Wild strawberry or Wood strawberry, botanically known as *Fragaria vesca*. Also, the Hautbois strawberry, *Fragaria elatior*, is mentioned by the well-known botanist of the sixteenth century, Gerarde. In the eighteenth century, the Alpine strawberry, *Fragaria alpina* was introduced from the continent of Europe into Britain and was subsequently grown extensively in gardens.

At that time, the North American strawberry, the Scarlet or Virginian strawberry, *Fragaria virginiana*, was introduced into Europe, and the Chili strawberry from Chile. They were, however, considered to be not as good as the native European strawberry, the Wood strawberry.

During the beginning of the eighteenth century, the present-day strawberries were developed by crossing the Virginian or Scarlet strawberry with the Chili strawberry. From these have developed the modern large-fruiting varieties which are now in cultivation.

Today, there appear to be three main types of strawberries in cultivation. The first is the Alpine, or small-fruiting types; the second the Large-fruiting varieties; and thirdly the Perpetual types.

The Alpine ones are noted for their free and continuous fruit-bearing quality, and also for their ease of cultivation. The Large-fruiting varieties are esteemed for their size and flavor. The Perpetuals are valued for their ability to supply berries throughout the summer and autumn. The Perpetuals, by the way, are a result of a cross between the Alpine and the Large-fruited kinds, and these strawberries are particularly popular.

Medicinal use of strawberries

Like the currants, strawberries have great medicinal value. They are said to be useful in the treatment of impure blood and also anemia, to improve low vitality or a low appetite, and for bowel and stomach disorders. But whatever their value to the body, they are certainly good to eat.

Rooting strawberry runners

15 Blueberries

Blueberries bear well in acid soils and have a long life.

These plants, also called whortleberry and bilberry, are present in acid moorland soils of North America, the British Isles, and across northern Europe and Asia, growing to 6–8 ft (2 m) tall and in large plantations. Wild berries are harvested, but are small. Modern cultivated blueberries are as large as small black grapes and begin to color early in summer, lasting for several weeks.

The fruits require an acid soil, like the azalea and rhododendron, so work plenty of peat moss about the roots at planting time, which is early spring. The plants also require plenty of nitrogenous manures to encourage the formation of a continuous supply of new wood upon which high quality fruit is obtained. Dig in rotted manure or composted straw. And in spring each year scatter on the surface around each plant 1 oz (28 g) of sulfate of potash and the same of superphosphate, mixed together. This will increase the quality of fruit. They should always be mulched.

Plant deeper than other fruits, as reproduction and new growth are by underground suckers, which may be detached and replanted to increase.

Set the plants 4 ft (120 cm) apart, for they grow bushy and at least 4 ft (120 cm) tall. Plants have a long life and bear heavily. The plants crop better if helped with their pollination, so plant two varieties together, one to give early crops, the other later. Three plants of each will provide worthwhile pickings. Blueberries turn from green to red then pale blue before turning black.

Varieties

Berkeley Huge berries of good quality. Ripens in midseason after Earliblue.

Bluecrop Bright colored, high quality berries. Requires pruning to slow down its remarkable productiveness. Midseason, ripening before Berkeley.

Blueray Large light blue berries of good flavor. Midseason, ripening about one week after Earliblue.

Darrow Medium-sized light blue berries. Fruit is very late, ripening one month after Earliblue.

Earliblue One of the earliest blueberries of high quality.

Herbert Very large berries produced in generous clusters. A later variety, ripening about 25 days after Earliblue.

Cranberries

This twiggy shrub grows to 2 ft (60 cm) tall in acid boglands. The plants form a dense mass of long wiry stems, and in September and October the fruits ripen to brightest crimson with a delicious sharp taste.

Plant only in low ground, for during summer its roots should be continually submerged in water. Plant 4 ft (120 cm) apart as it spreads quickly. Propagation is by lifting and dividing the roots in winter.

16 Rhubarb

Though a vegetable, rhubarb is always used as a fruit. As it can be forced during winter in warmth or in the open, it is one of the most valuable crops, and the first outdoor rhubarb always enjoys a welcome. It may be grown in light shade where little else will grow. It will also grow well in any soil. It requires plenty of humus to maintain summer moisture if it is to make those thick, juicy sticks so much in demand for stewing or for pies and tarts. So dig in plenty of rotted manure or garden compost and give the roots a mulch in summer.

Many gardeners treat rhubarb as a decorative feature, positioning it where the large leaves can be seen, and also where the stems can be harvested without the need to tramp over wet soil.

In addition, why not set a clump of these plants as exclamation marks at the ends of rows of asparagus? Here, again, they will be easily accessible when harvesting time comes around. Fortunately, the soil preparation for asparagus exactly suits the needs of the rhubarb – making a happy combination.

Rhubarb roots, or thongs, must contain an 'eye', which will produce a stalk. Without this there will be no plant. The roots are planted in fall or spring while dormant, for they begin to grow with the first warm spring sunshine. Plant 2 ft (60 cm) apart with the 'eye' or bud just below soil level,

Rhubarb is a popular vegetable that is always used as a fruit.

but make the hole deep enough to take the long root.

At planting time, give a 4 oz per sq yd (132 g per sq m) dressing of basic slag, which rhubarb loves, for it releases its nitrogen content over a long time.

Pull no stalks the first year and only a few in the second year. By then, the roots will be established and a dozen stalks or more can be removed in the year.

After four years the roots will have grown to 18 in (45 cm) across. To prevent them becoming too hard and woody, lift in fall and divide with a knife or spade, remembering that each piece of root must have at least one 'eye'. Treat the cut parts with lime or flowers of sulphur before replanting.

Producing early crops

If there are several roots, one or two can be lifted and forced in a garage or beneath the greenhouse bench. But first allow it to remain for a week or two in the open after lifting during cold, even freezing, weather; this will make it force all the better. Half fill a deep orange crate with a friable soil (a mixture of loam, peat and decayed manure is ideal), and in it place the root with the 'eye' at soil level. Water in and place a sheet of cardboard or a sack over the top to exclude light. If planted in December, the stalks, reddish-pink in color, will have reached to the covering by the end of January. They will be about 12–15 in (30–37 cm) long and are then removed as required by pulling. Use the largest first to allow the others to grow on. When cropping has finished, turn out the roots, divide them and re-plant in spring to grow on, but do not remove any stalks that year.

Another way to obtain early stalks is to cover a mature root in the open where it is growing. This is done by placing over it a deep box or upturned bucket. The previous year's stalks will have died back during winter. Before covering, place over the root some fresh strawy manure or composted straw, which will provide some warmth. About March 1 is the time to cover the roots, and the first stalks will be ready to pull about mid-April.

Uncovered roots outdoors will produce stalks to use in early May and they will continue for a few weeks. Rhubarb freezes well. Late in autumn, remove the old stalks and foliage, dig over the soil around the roots and give a strawy mulch.

Varieties

Canada Red It forces well outdoors and bears large, thick, red stalks right through summer.

Valentine Known for its bright red stalks.

Victoria Stalks are red on the outside, green within. Very vigorous.

Below left: Divide long-established rhubarb roots in winter before re-planting into well-manured ground.

Below: Rhubarb can be forced by covering the roots in January with pots or boxes in order to draw up the stalks.

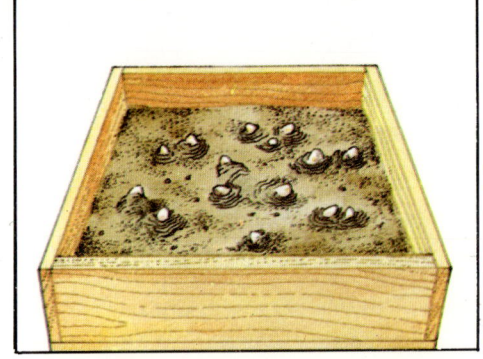

17 Pests and diseases

Apple

Aphid It feeds on the young shoots and leaves, causing them to curl up, and early in winter it lays on the spurs. To control, spray with malathion after petals fall.

Codling moth A serious pest, the tiny white grubs of which burrow into the fruits leaving a pile of brown dirt at the entrance hole. Spray with rotenone each month after petals fall from June to September to control.

Scab It attacks shoots, leaves and fruits as black blisters. The home gardener should select varieties least susceptible to the disease. Spraying with captan, manels or ferbam as part of a regular spraying will help.

Blackberry

Cane spot Attacks all cane fruits, usually in a cold, wet summer, as brown spots on canes and leaves, which fall. Spray in spring, before flowers open, with Bordeaux mixture.

Cherry

Canker It affects mostly black cherries, first as yellow leaf spots, causing leaves to fall, later as brown areas on branches. Spray with Bordeaux mixture – 1 lb (500 g) copper sulphate and ¾ lb (375 g) slaked lime to 6 gall (30 liters) of water in spring before buds open.

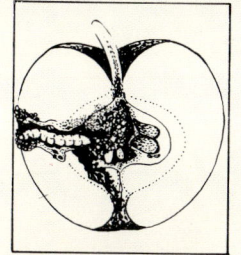

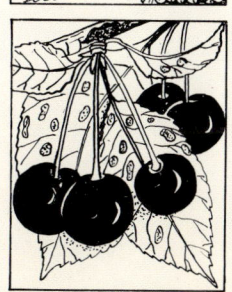

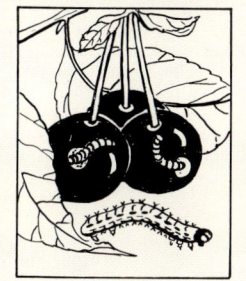

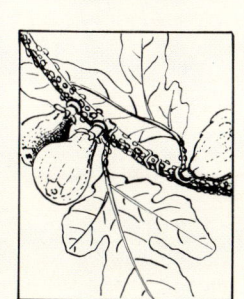

Cherry (cont.)

Aphid The tiny black eggs winter on the twigs; the grubs, on hatching in spring, feed on the leaves and new growth. Control by routine spraying with malathion as part of general spray program.

Fruit moth The small green caterpillars enter the flower buds and later bore into the fruits, making them uneatable. The fruits fall, the moths emerging in spring to lay their eggs on the blossom. Dust with rotenone just before the blossom opens.

Fig

Scale It also attacks vines, apricots and peaches, appearing as white scale-like insects, clustering on the stems and sucking the sap. To control, spray with malathion in early March.

Peach

Leaf curl The most troublesome disease, attacking the leaves and causing them to curl. Later, they take on a powdery look and die. Spraying with ferbam or 8–8–10 Bordeaux before buds begin to swell will control to some extent.

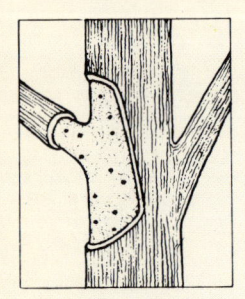

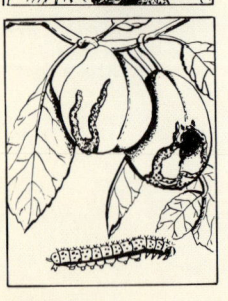

Peach (cont.)

Borers Borers infest trunks and branches, often after winter injury or pruning scars have been made. Borers can be removed with a wire or knife. Borers in the trunk are killed by paradichlorobenzene crystals applied around the base of the trunk.

Pear

Fire blight Also attacks apple and quince. New growth appears to be scorched by fire, the change often occurring very quickly. Plant resistant varieties. Cut off infected branches; spray with an antibiotic, Actidione.

Scab Though the symptoms are similar in appearance, scab on pears takes a different form from that which attacks apples. Spray with captan or ferbam early in May and again after blossom set, early in June.

Plum and gage

Brown rot It attacks the fruit spurs, the blossom (as blossom wilt) and later the fruits, causing them to mummify on the trees. To control it, remove mummified fruit in winter. Spray with captan after petals fall.

Sawfly As well as plums and gages, it attacks apples and gooseberries when in bloom, laying on the flower buds, the white caterpillars causing the buds to die. Spray with methoxychlor; apples at petal fall, plums ten days later; or use rotenone and a spreader.

Plum and gage (cont.)

Silver leaf Its presence is shown by the leaves taking on a silver appearance and the trees soon die. It enters through cuts. For this reason, pruning should be completed by mid-July so that the cuts will 'gum' quickly. There is no known cure.

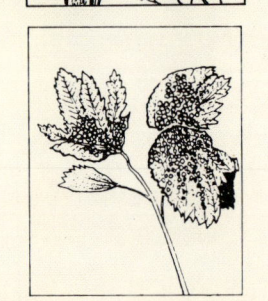

Raspberry

Raspberry beetle It also attacks blackberries and loganberries, laying its eggs on the flowers. After hatching, the white grubs eat into the fruits. To prevent, spray with rotenone as the flowers open and again when the fruit has set.

Raspberry moth It winters in the soil and emerges in spring as a silver-brown moth to lay its eggs on the flowers. The caterpillars eat the fruits, often entirely. To prevent, dust with rotenone as for raspberry beetle.

Red and white currants

Aphid Can be common on currants. Spray with malathion as leaf buds are unfurling.

Strawberry

Aphid It feeds on the sap and reduces vigor, allowing virus diseases to enter at the punctures. To control, spray with Malathion before the blossoms open.

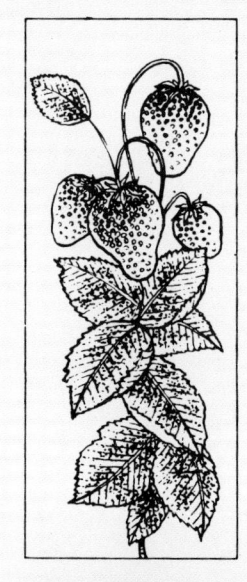

Mites Most troublesome of strawberry pests, both the cyclamen and two-spotted mites can infest plants. Severely stunted plants should be destroyed. Spraying with Kelthane, making several applications 10–14 days apart, will check the mites before they cause serious damage.

Botrytis (mildew) Both are forms of mildew, botrytis attacking the fruits, mildew the foliage, as a powdery white fungus. Dust with 10% captan, as soon as the first green fruits have set.

Red stele Caused by a fungus that attacks the roots, causing them to turn red at the center and the plants to die back. There is no cure, so, in low-lying, badly drained land, plant in raised beds or plant resistant varieties.

Note: The best way to control the various pests and diseases of fruit trees is to use a general purpose fruit spray several times during the growing season. Directions for the timing of the sprays are usually on the container, but such information, along with information on the pests common to a particular region, can be obtained from the county extension specialist.

Although regulations regarding pesticides are being constantly reviewed, the major chemicals in fruit sprays are malathion, captan, methoxychlor and sometimes carbaryl.

The US Department of Agriculture has published a booklet, *Control of Insects on Deciduous Fruits and Tree Nuts in the Home Orchard Without Insecticides*. It is Home and Garden Bulletin No. 211 and can be obtained from the Superintendent of Document, US Government Printing Office, Washington, DC 20402.

Index

aphis, 61, 63
apples, 8–15
  frost-resistance, 6, 14, 15
  harvesting and storing, 12–13
  pests and diseases, 61
  planting, 9–10
  pollination, 9
  preparation of ground, 6
  site, 4
  soil requirements, 8–9
  training and pruning, 10–12
  varieties, 13–15
apricots, 30–31

bacterial canker, 27, 61
beetle, raspberry, 63
blackberries, 43–45
  pests and diseases, 61
  preparation of the soil, 44
  propagation, 44
  site, 5, 43
  soil requirements, 6, 44
  varieties, 45
blackcurrants, 51–53
  frost-resistance, 6, 51, 52, 53
  pests and diseases, 61
  planting, 51
  preparation of soil, 51
  pruning, 51–52
  site, 5, 51
  soil requirements, 6, 51
  varieties, 52–53
black fly, 62
blossom weevil, 61
blossom wilt, 61
blueberries, 58
botrytis, 63
brown rot, 63
bullaces, 26

cane spot, 61
cherries, 27–29
  pests and diseases, 6, 61–62
  pollination, 28–29
  pruning, 28
  soil requirements, 6, 27
  varieties, 29
chlorosis, 6
clearwing moth, 63
codling moth, 61
cranberries, 58
currants, 51–53
  black, 5, 6, 51–53
  frost-resistance, 6, 51, 52, 53
  pests and diseases, 61, 63
  planting, 51
  preparation of soil, 51
  pruning, 51–52
  red, 5, 53
  site, 5, 51, 53
  soil requirements, 6, 51
  varieties, 52–53
  white, 53

damsons, 26
  site, 4, 26
  varieties, 26
diseases, 61–63

fertilizers, 6, 7
figs, 38–39
  harvesting and storing, 39
  pests and diseases, 62
  planting, 38
  propagation, 39
  pruning, 38–39
  varieties, 39
fruit moth, 62

gages, 21–25
  harvesting and storing, 23
  pests and diseases, 6, 63
  pollination, 23
  root pruning, 22–23
  rootstocks, 23
  site, 4
  soil requirements, 23
  training and pruning, 21–22
  varieties, 24–25
gall mite, 61
gooseberries, 47–50
  pests and diseases, 62
  planting, 48
  preparing the soil, 48
  propagation, 49–50
  pruning, 48
  site, 4–5, 47
  varieties, 50
grapes, 33–37
  pests and diseases, 62
  planting, 34
  propagation, 36
  pruning, 34–36
  site, 5, 33
  varieties, 36
greenfly, 61, 63

humus, 6, 7

leaf curl, 62
liming, 6–7
loganberries, 5, 46

manure, 6, 7
mealy bug, 62
midge, 62
mildew, 62, 63
moths, 61, 62, 63

nectarines, 32

peaches, 31–32
  pests and diseases, 62
  pruning, 31–32
  site, 4, 31
  varieties, 32

pears, 16–20
  espalier, 4, 16–17
  frost-resistance, 6
  harvesting and storing, 19
  pests and diseases, 62
  pollination, 17
  pruning, 18
  rootstocks, 18–19
  site, 4, 16
  varieties, 19–20
pests, 61–63
planning the fruit garden, 4–7
plums, 21–25
  frost-resistance, 6, 21
  harvesting and storing, 23
  pests and diseases, 6, 63
  pollination, 23
  root pruning, 22–23
  rootstocks, 23
  site, 4
  soil requirements, 6, 23
  training and pruning, 21–22
  varieties, 24–25

raspberries, 40–42
  frost-resistance, 6, 40
  pests and diseases, 63
  planting, 41
  preparing the ground, 41
  site, 5, 40
  varieties, 42
raspberry beetle, 63
raspberry moth, 63
red core, 63
redcurrants, 53
  pests and diseases, 63
  site, 5, 53
  varieties, 53
rhubarb, 59–60
rust, 61

sawfly, 63
scab, 61, 62
scale, 62
silver leaf, 21, 27, 63
soils, types of, 6–7
strawberries, 54–57
  autumn-fruiting, 56
  growing in tubs, 56
  pests and diseases, 63
  planting, 55–56
  preparing the soil, 55
  site, 5
  varieties, 55–56

vines, 5, 33–37
vine weevil, 62

weevils, 61, 62
white currants, 53
  pests and diseases, 63
winter moth, 61